Sell Me a Prayer

Sheila Bosire

Stories from **Canon Literature Media**

Sell Me a Prayer

Sheila Bosire

Canon
Literature Media
Reading is True

Published by
Canon Literature Media
Nyayo Est. Embakasi, Apt. 68, Court 190
P. O. Box 12773 - 00100
Nairobi, Kenya.

First Published 2018

For Bishop Oscar Muriu, Nairobi Chapel
In loving memory of Bishop James Ocholla
To all those who have given their lives
to sincere Christian service

Prologue

Defined simply as "communication with God or a deity", prayer is an activity dating back to the very beginning of civilisations. The Judaism scriptures and consequently the Bible,, record that man did communicate with his God from the very beginning. This communication did not take the form of prayer then but rather a face to face kind of fellowship until the fall of man and consequently creation. After this disconnect resulted, man resorted to prayer, speaking with his deity from a distance. The exact time is recorded as the times when a character known as Enosh, a son, was born to Seth. Seth was the son who was born to Adam and Eve, the first family, after the murder of Abel. (Gen 4:26 - *And as for Seth, to him also a son was born; and he named him Enosh. Then men began to call on the name of the Lord.*)

The necessity of prayer stems from the fact that man, in the end, is finite, limited, weak and mortal. Often he finds that he has to grapple with several issues; some as simple as where to find his next meal; the weather and the need for it to be favourable for his survival his own weaknesses, those he loves and is attached to; the larger scheme of things like a favourable political regime, perhaps to escape incidences like the holocaust, wars, genocide, religious extremism, and who knows what?

It may be argued that, primarily, it is not that man loves his God that he prays but rather his cognisance of the fact that he needs his God. Prayer cuts across race, class, colour or creed and eventually man will pray not only because he needs his God for his preservation and subsistence but for his very joy, perhaps. It is an activity found among the rich, healthy and prosperous, just as it is found among the poor and scum. It is as if man is incomplete without this constant communication and guidance from his God. To put it simply, when all problems disappear from the face of the earth then prayer too will disappear.

In the beginning, everything is said to have been perfect, this was God's intention for His creation; a perfect life. Human beings have from then on been in the pursuit of a perfect life; a life where one's activities bring fulfilment and joy. It has been argued that according to the good book, since the creator made man in His own image, He should be able to take full charge of affairs on earth immediately and end the misery and evil that many encounter in this world.

However, isn't it is ironic that a parent similarly gives birth to a child and though the child is initially dependent on the parent, he eventually acquires a life of his own and grows into full adult maturity? Although a parent may want to exercise control over their offspring when the decisions and directions they take as adults are contrary to treasured values, it is impossible to do so. The parent can advise and only hope that their child will take heed and choose good over evil. Many times, the parent is left to nurse a broken heart and though it hurts he has to come to the realisation and resolution that in the end, every human being has the divine privilege of choice. In the end the parent's role was only to transmit and nurture life to another human being. He or she has no control. He is similarly a child and as varied and different as we may be in this world, it is said that we are all children of one father.

It is recorded in the Bible that indeed God has in the past taken full charge of the occurrences on earth, resulting in the decision to preserve one family, the family of Noah. Noah happened to be the only human being left with Godly attributes; attributes pleasing to his father. Attributes that perpetuate life, like love, tenderness, diligence, kindness, honesty, chastity, and so on. Even then, he had the task of convincing fellow men to change their conduct or else a flood would come and drown every living thing. It is recorded that it was a hard decision for God to destroy all unrepentant men through a flood; that His heart was full of regret. The maker of the universe was broken hearted.

> *Now the LORD observed the extent of the people's wickedness, and he saw that all their thoughts were consistently and totally evil. (Gen 6:5 NLT)*
>
> *So the LORD was sorry he had ever made them. It broke his heart. (Gen 6:6 NLT)*
>
> *And the LORD said, "I will completely wipe out this human race that I have created. Yes, and I will destroy all the animals and birds, too. I am sorry I ever made them." (Gen 6:7 NLT)*
>
> *But Noah found favour with the LORD. (Gen 6:8 NLT)*

Another incident when God took full charge was when another city, Sodom, had to be destroyed because, similarly, they had lost all sense of the attributes that nurture life. In this case, nobody was found worthy to be spared except one stranger named Lot who had settled among the locals. He was evacuated along with his family and the city was destroyed with all in it by fire as recorded in Gen.19:1-29.

Historically then, it is preferable when man in his moral and other limitations works in partnership with his God in order to make life worth living. It is a law that cannot be broken, since God will not intervene in anything in man's domain unless man asks him to.

Prayer has therefore been a constant conversation between man and his God for the thousands of years that the earth has existed.

Noel Karo, the son of a preacher Rev. Jay Karo, counts himself lucky to have been familiar with the story since his childhood. It was the story of a God who delighted in his creation and who obeys his own rules. Man has no control over the sunrise in the morning- or the sunset at dusk. He has no direct control of the seasons; when they should commence or end. He has no choice of where to be born, which race to be born in, nationality or gender. His creator has control over these things. The best man can do is find out the mechanisms and laws of the universe and their workings. Although science has proved its ability to alter and control some situations, it always has to work with what is already provided. An invention though brilliant, is in itself dependent on research of existing laws, atoms, materials, chemical components and so on. It is therefore in his intricate affairs that man needs the intervention of his God and therefore he resorts to communicating with him through prayer.

Chapter 1

❀

The house was filled with an aroma of delicious food, tinkling of cutlery and glasses, carefree chatter, and warm laughter. The atmosphere was ignited with a deep, solid, irrefutable feeling of wellbeing. Rev. Jay Karo's friends, neighbours and colleagues from all walks of life had gathered in his home to celebrate his birthday. The party extended to the lawn with chairs and parasols and children running from one end to another. Rev. Jay's wife and children had arranged a surprise birthday party to celebrate the milestone of his attaining seventy years. Forty of these years were spent in service as a pastor. Rev. Jay had been totally unaware of these arrangements.

*****

They drove from the barber's shop. His younger son, Noel, had tricked him into leaving the house by 8:30am for a shave, a swim and breakfast at his favourite coffee house. Later, he had driven his dad to his house and laid out some clothes which his mother had picked out for him to change.

"You got me clothes to change?" Rev. Jay asked his son, "What's the use since I am heading home anyway? You'll drop me off, won't you?"

"Yes Dad, I will. But I just wanted you to feel comfortable since you already took a shower after our workout," he answered.

"I am okay son," Rev. Jay insisted, "I had this extra t-shirt I have changed into but if you insist ..."

Just then Noel's wife stepped into the room and kissed her father-in-law on the cheek. "Happy birthday Papa!" she sang. "How are you feeling?" She greeted him.

Rev. Jay smiled at Sherry, his daughter-in-law. As usual, Sherry was so unconventional: she was an artist and she loved colourful things. She was wearing a long bright pink blouse, lime green cotton pants with huge dangling blue earrings.

"I am well, thank you, Sherry, and you?" he replied.

"I am good; we are all good, thanking God for this daaay Papa!"she said excitedly.

Noel led his father to the guest room. His three year old son ran towards his grandfather, followed at a distance by their five year old daughter. Rev. Jay gathered the little boy in his arms and gave him a kiss as Sherry gently took him from his arms.

"It's grandpa's birthday today," she said to little John, "Let him change into his best clothes first!"

Rev. Jay lifted up their daughter Miriam too and gave her a kiss.

"Happy birthday grandpa," she said softly.

"Thank you Mama¹," Rev. Jay said to his granddaughter.

Noel opened the door to the guest room where his father's clothes were laid out.

"You go ahead Dad," he said and shut the door behind him.

---

1   Mama – a common way of expressing endearment
     in Kenyan culture when referring to little girls by
     their elders, adapted from the Swahili culture.

*****

A half an hour later, at 1:00 p.m., Noel drove his young family and his dad to his parent's home. "What! Balloons?" Rev. Jay exclaimed as they approached the driveway. There were large, blue and white balloons hoisted high on either side of the gate. On each side of the driveway, there were three blue and white streamers, with the number 70 on them, fluttering in the wind within a few metres intervals.

"You went all the way to outdo yourself, didn't you?" Rev. Jay asked jestingly. Noel and Sherry feigned surprise.

"I don't know anything about this!" Noel replied, tongue-in-cheek. Little John shouted, "It's grandpa's birthday!"

They drove into the compound to a gathered reception. The secret was out. Everybody in the house had come out to join those outside and together they sang:

Happy birthday to you,
Happy birthday to you,
Happy birthday Rev Jay!
Happy birthday to you!

Mrs Magadalina Karo, Rev. Jay's wife, stepped forward and gave him a kiss and a hug. "Happy birthday my dear," she said. Soon, his elder son Chris, his daughters Neema[2], Sarah and May followed. Many others followed suit. As surprised as he was, Rev. Jay's joy could be felt as some of the members of his congregation congratulated him and wished him well. His face lit up when he saw some friends and relations whom he had not seen for a while, some of whom had travelled to make this

---

2   Neema - literally "Grace", is a Swahili equivalent
      of the English female name Grace.

day memorable to him. It was a house full of joy and there was a band playing light music on the lawn, mostly his favourites: some hymns, some gospel country music, and some upbeat contemporary Christian music which his children had played in his house during their teenage years. He had come to love them and he couldn't help but smile at the recollection.

Among the many people, his eyes could pick out the long term members of the church. His son Noel's close friends had also come. There was Sheba and her husband Eric. Their house help Mimo was serving drinks. Further along were George and her husband Michael with their three children. Their house help Eusebia was holding a tray with cutlery. Salome and her children were present as well, all busy doing something. The pastors, board of deacons, and church elders were of course present. Jabali More, a well-known politician and Rev. Jay's childhood friend, had honoured the invitation. Teresa was further along and, surprisingly, Jabali's son, Samba More, and his wife Natasha were present too among about 200 of the invited guests.

Rev. Jay was a tall man, about six feet tall, with dark chocolate complexion and kind, intelligent eyes. His greying hair and unruffled manner gave him a dignified air though unobtrusive. He was one of those people who gave those around him and those who approached him a feeling of safety and trustworthiness. There was a table indoors where his close friends and relations – about nine – who had travelled to celebrate his birthday sat and food was served.

Rev. Jay's heart was so full. All he could think about was God's faithfulness to good old Jay Karo, as that is what he considered himself first. Jay Karo, a guy born to a simple village family, privileged to get an education and better still, privileged to have parents who had embraced the Christian faith and lifestyle.

Their conversation went on and on as they not only caught up with Jay but with each other as they ate. In an hour and a half's time, the music went off and the master of ceremony for the party spoke up and quieted everyone down. It was time to cut the cake and he called Rev. Jay to the lawn where a large, three-tiered white forest cake with seven candles had been placed.

Little John defied his mother's restraints and pressed himself onto his grandfather, jumping into his arms the minute he stretched them out. Together, they cut the cake and everyone sang the birthday song followed by a rendition of the hymn "Great is thy Faithfulness"[3] backed up by the band. Immediately after the hymn, there was the sound of flutes, drums and shakers as a group of musicians who were hitherto in the house came out singing the famous coastal tune,

> *Nakupenda kama sukari*
> *Nakwambia kweli si siri*
> *Ningekuwa mimi tajiri*
> *Ningekununulia gari!*[4]

Rev. Jay Karo shook his shoulders to the traditional rhythm. He smiled widely and engaged in a series of jigs to humour the guests. Later, when was asked to say a word, he mainly gave thanks for God's faithfulness to him, his family and the larger congregation he had been a pastor to for the past years. The

---

3   Full hymn at the back.
4   *I love you like sugar*
     I am letting you know, it's no secret
     If I were a rich man
     I would buy you a car

5

party continued and some of his friends were given a chance to say something to and about Jay on his birthday. Many had brought him presents in cash and in kind. Later on in the evening, the guests began to leave. Eusebia, Mimo, Salome and her children as well as the party caterers were still busy serving tea, coffee, drinks and snacks for those who lingered on.

Being a hot January night and having been in a state of exhilaration the large part of the day, Rev. Jay found it difficult to go to sleep at night. He got up from his bed, took a glass of water, and quietly stepped out of his bedroom onto the balcony. As he sat there, he felt cooler and his thoughts became contemplative. He couldn't help but remember how difficult his journey had been at first. He was born into a poor village family. His earliest memories included how much he valued his bowl of porridge and his meals generally, which he would sometimes do without. He could recall going without a meal once in a while when the harvest had been really bad and what they had had to stretch over a certain period of time. To him, the missionaries were a godsend and similarly his father's attitude towards what they had to offer. His father had embraced both formal education and Christianity, sending all his children to school. Jay had been enrolled in school at the age of nine and had turned out to be a brilliant student. The missionaries then were not only eager to make converts but to convince some into lifelong service in religion and the church as nuns, priests and pastors.

As life continued, Jay had embraced education, appreciating its enabling and enlightening role. It dispelled baseless notions and beliefs held for centuries which belonged in the realm of superstition and fortified solid, proven ways. And where education had failed, Christianity had provided an answer.

Life had become more tolerable after joining school because they would be served a meal and sometimes tea. He had struck rapport with the head teacher, Mr Gordon Snow, who sometimes allowed him to slash the compound in exchange for a three-shilling wage. However, independence came and with it a change in everything. There was an exodus among the white people who couldn't imagine living in a country governed by Africans and for a short while as things transitioned, the fate of their school was in doubt. Mr Snow left for England and was replaced by an African. Mr Snow gave Jay his address in England. The two contemporaries communicated through letters and rare phone calls over the years.

Having been fascinated by numbers for most of his life, his first degree was in business management, specialising in accounts. Two years later after graduating, he had taken up a master's degree in divinity in England, recommended by Mr Snow.

As he sat on a cane chair at the balcony, Rev. Jay struggled with his thoughts. He had begun his calling as a pastor, without much and relying on his meagre allowance from the mission. He had learnt then the intricacies of finance and how difficult things could get. He had to learn self-control as a pastor and to understand his place whenever he would be attending to somebody who had more material possessions and wasn't struggling to meet his needs like he was. He had to learn how to relate with those who had more power and influence in society, in need of his guidance, without being intimidated. He met folks from various walks of life and used the Bible to learn nuggets of wisdom on how to handle everybody and anybody. He also had to learn how to succeed in his work. His greatest point of reference however, as he often told his son Noel, had been to always remember that it was God who was in charge and who had called him to Christian service and not men. He was a servant to fellow human beings but they were not his master, God was, and that was what gave him much comfort and security. He held the promise in Matt. 16:18 *"And I tell you that you are Peter, and on this rock I will build my church, and the gates of Hades will not overcome it."* He felt that though he may fail many times, with this promise, he would be a winner in the final analysis.

In those initial years, Pastor Jay had encountered a long stretch of near poverty and a lack of results in his ministry. Now as he thought of his son, whose life had been much easier than his, he wondered what kind of minister he would become if he too lived to be seventy years of age or more. He felt deeply disturbed when he read about various cases of sham preachers in the local press and the shameful acts they committed. These preachers' lives were devoid of what could be considered a testimony. They lacked patience, which is the key to bearing lasting fruit. They also lead many astray. Christian service had been difficult, entailing fasting, long hours in prayer, studying, visiting various homes, accommodating some in one's home, false accusations, the lure of pride, the constant need for money and other challenges. The society held high moral standards for a pastor and expected him to be beyond reproach. Rev. Jay knew that he was only an instrument in God's hands and that he could not rely on his own ability.

He thought of Woodlands City Congregation Adams Arcade area, along Ngong Road, the church he had the privilege to pastor much like a large, fruitful garden. It consisted of various fruit trees and decorative trees. It had various herbs, berry bushes and numerous blooming flowers in colourful hues. However, it had taken a lot of work and time to develop and tend the garden to its present state. It would take even more work and dedication over the years to come, not only to maintain the garden but to improve it and make it more pleasant and fruitful; a garden where the weary soul could find shelter, reprieve and nourishment. The church had grown to have about three thousand members, many of whom were in families and had children. There were times when pests and snakes had found their way into this garden but God, "the Great Gardener" as Rev. Jay referred to him, always took charge and helped the church get rid of them.

Noel, had followed after his father Rev. Jay, and apart from a few years of near rebellion in his teenage, he had always admired his father. It came as a surprise to Rev. Jay though when Noel, upon being convinced that he too had a calling, decided to follow after his father; deciding to pursue Bible studies. He had gone ahead to do so in the United States where he eventually met his wife. Among his children, Rev. Jay would have thought that his elder son would have been the one to take up after him. They were more alike. However, Chris, his elder son, had decided to pursue an engineering career and had become a successful practising engineer with a family of his own.

A smile softened his countenance when he remembered that Noel seemed to be handling things very well so far. He still kept a watchful eye on him but by and large, his son had control and had taken up the responsibility of being the lead pastor of the church. He had adapted well to the elders and deacons of the church and treated them with respect during their meetings. He had an easy disposition and had been a sociable person right from his childhood.

9

It is amazing how life flies by. Have I made my days count? Rev. Jay pondered. *I will never know until I get to the other side but I know I am doing my best and keeping the faith. I hope that's good enough.*

From time to time, Rev. Jay travelled with his son Noel and one more pastor at a time to the villages, five in total, where they had begun outreach projects and support. Sometimes it was school books that they needed to restock and other times there was need to drill a borehole. The people on the ground had come to know Rev. Jay but were pleasantly surprised to see his grown son. "It is an exciting moment when a generation succeeds their forefathers," one elder had remarked. During these times, they would live the village life alongside the villagers. Sometimes there was need to help purchase a donkey to help in drawing water from a borehole for the pastor and his household or staff. Initially, they had taught them how to improve in their farming activities.

Every human being and community had their honour and way of bestowing it to those who they identify with as kin and friend. Rev. Jay Karo had been privileged to such occasions which he treasured in his heart. At times, the villagers wanted to share a delicacy, a meal indigenous to their area and community. There were other times when it would be singing besides a bonfire or when a traditional piece of clothing or artefact would be gifted to him. These were earthly rewards that warmed his heart and lifted his spirit. The changing lives in the community deeply touched him. There were also two smaller branches of the main church. Sun City Congregation was in another part of the city, and Palm City Congregation was located in the coastal City of Mombasa. Noel's elder sister, Neema, and her family attended the Sun City Congregation in Mombasa where she had settled. Though she was an accountant by profession, she was also in charge of the music at the church.

Noel had learnt that time in a pastor's life was extremely precious; especially one that had a sizeable congregation to take care of. Rev. Jay had told his son of those first days in his work when there wasn't as much work and sometimes all he would do on successive days would be praying and studying and conducting weekly services. Sometimes, nobody would be in need of counselling for close to a month. The key to growth was remaining focused on his mission and being in touch with the community in all seasons to reach out whenever there was need as well as when all seemed to be okay.

Rev. Jay had shared his thoughts on appointing Noel to succeed him with his wife Magadalina as well as Elder Andreaand his wife. He had asked them to give him their opinion on the matter after one week. Though he had felt confident that Noel was going to make it as a pastor and leader, he had felt that it would be good to confer with those who were close to him. After one month, they had met in the boardroom one evening and his wife, Magadalina Karo, and Elder Andrea and his wife had confirmed that they believed it was okay for Noel to lead the church after him. They had also discussed what role Pastor Seth should play. Pastor Seth was Rev. Jay's assistant over the years.

After their meeting Rev. Jay Karo had had a dinner meeting with Pastor Seth and had shared his thoughts on the future of Woodlands City Congregation and its associated church branches and missions. After they had spoken for a long period of time and had their dinner, they prayed. Pastor Seth had seemed to receive the news well and had supported Rev. Jay's decision. With that, a meeting with the board of elders and deacons had been arranged in order to communicate to them the news on their decision and to also obtain their endorsement. The board of elders and deacons had held short meetings weekly and a longer meeting once a month on Saturday afternoons to deliberate on issues. During one of the longer meetings, Elder Andrea and Rev. Jay had communicated the decision to ordain pastor Noel as the leader of the Woodlands City Congregation church and its missions. The board of elders and deacons had then given their varied opinions on the matter. They had a one week period to think over the matter and during their next weekly meeting, they would relay their decision.

*****

Although Noel had graduated in his theological studies and had worked at the church, he had never been officially ordained. Rev. Jay and Elder Andrea thought about the matter separately and after a couple of days, Elder Andrea discussed the issue with Rev. Jay. They decided that they would have an ordination service for pastor Noel as soon as the board communicated their decision which they believed would be favourable. Although Rev. Jay and Pastor Seth would still be active, more room would be given to Pastor Noel and the team of pastors to do their work. Pastor Seth would take on more supervisory roles as well since Rev. Jay would be travelling out of the country, sometimes for longer periods.

Three months later, Noel and Sherry Karo were gathered with most of their friends from home as well as abroad. The decision to have Noel charting the course forward for Woodlands City Congregation had successfully sailed through with three-quarters of the board of elders and deacons endorsing it and only a quarter of the board being unsure about it. Those that had been unsure now supported the majority and were all in attendance as the service began.

*****

Noel Karo stood straight in his new pinstriped suit, a gift from his sisters May and Sarah, both of whom lived away in the United States and had travelled back to witness their brother's ordination service. Sarah was married to an American while May, the last born, was not yet married. With all eyes on him, Noel's looks presently stood out more distinctly different than those of his father. He was very light skinned like his mother and a little shorter than Rev. Jay, about five feet five inches tall. To the onlooker, he came across as young and inexperienced. The worship began and then a guest musician also sang before it was time to introduce Noel and his family to the gathering. Many of Rev. Jay's friends and associates had responded to his invitation to the ordination. The church auditorium was filled up to capacity. Elder Andrea and the music pastor jointly led the service. The music pastor read a short history on Noel's family background, religious conviction, education, experience and vision. Soon, Elder Andrea called Noel and his family - his wife Sherry and their children Miriam and John - to the pulpit and introduced them to the congregation.

Sherry and the children then went back to their seats as Rev. Jay and the Principal of Bible School who had travelled for this occasion stepped up to the pulpit. Rev. Jay introduced him to the congregation as Rev. David Thompson and a mentor to his son Noel before he went back to his seat. Rev. Thompson spoke encouraging words about Noel and his character and passion. He also spoke a few words on the calling into ministry and the issues that come with it. Money, women and power were singled out as potential dangers to him and his service as a pastor, if not handled well within the limits of the Bible and the accompanying code of ethics of a minister.

"Money in the end is a tool and how it is used is symbolic of what is most important to an individual, an organisation or a church. Through money, God can either be glorified or dishonoured. As long as you are in this world, you cannot escape handling money, only be careful and ask God to help you handle it with integrity," he said. Rev. Thompson called upon the board of elders and deacons to come onto the pulpit as well in order to ordain Noel and pray for him. They gathered round him as he knelt and Rev. Thompson, Rev. Jay and his wife Magadalina, Pastor Seth, and Elder Andrea laid their hands on him. After a series of prayers, Noel Karo got up and was announced as a bona fide minister of the gospel of Jesus Christ and the lead pastor of Woodlands City Congregation and its associated missions. The congregation clapped and cheered. Noel was then given a few minutes to speak before the service was brought to a conclusion as the choir sang.

*****

At Rev. Jay's residence, lunch had been prepared to serve about five hundred guests. Rev. Jay's house was a moderate yet beautiful four-bedroomed house and the compound was extensive enough to hold a large number of guests. Later, when everybody left, Rev. Jay and Noel sat at the patio and enjoyed a cup of evening tea.

"There was a time Noel, my son, when being a pastor was quite an honour in the community and wider society," Rev. Jay solemnly spoke, "but I am not sure that is always the case today. It seems that some of us referred to by that name have dishonoured the call and profession. Today, only one's actions over time determine whether one is truly staying true to their call. Therefore, guard your honour. Remember that God is always watching and He will forever remain your help," he told his son.

Chapter 2

❋

Noel Karo was still elated in the afterglow of his ordination. The ceremony had been well attended by Jay's associates as well as Noel's friends and family, church members and prominent persons from various walks of life. He stared at the picture of him and his father on his office desk. Rev. Jay Karo had lost some weight in the past few months of his life. *It must be due to the travelling and the rush of activities he has been engaged in,* Noel thought. Lately, Rev. Jay had been resting more due to back pain and had retreated to the Coast with his wife for a while. His appetite had also been wanting as was characteristic of him during excessively busy periods. During such times, Noel's mother had to strictly prevail on him to eat healthy meals in good proportions and to take some time off to rest.

Rev. Jay had been was like a strong oak to many, beginning with his family members and his son Noel. Noel was assured that at least he would spend many days with his father, receiving counsel, reproof and commendation. He worked on the following year's calendar of activities which had been brought to his office for changes including additions or subtractions to the slotted events and his general approval. The calendar of activities was usually done in November of the preceding year after collecting information and proposals from the various departments of the church. The pastoral team, elders, deacons and supporting church staff would then pray about the proposed activities for about a week and subsequently retreat to a location for about four days where they would thresh through all the propositions. After all the work was done, the senior pastor would also be given some leeway to amend the calendar and confirm the changes with the other pastors. It was on a Friday that Noel was supposed to hand over the changes to the secretary who would issue the same to other pastors, but Noel withheld his changes for a few more days as he waited for Rev. Jay to come back to Nairobi so that they could discuss them.

*****

Rev. Jay and his wife had come back as expected; however, Rev. Jay was feeling even worse than he had felt before leaving for the trip. When they arrived, they found the family, his children and grandchildren, already gathered in the house and a big dinner was. Such a gathering especially warmed Rev. Jay's heart; it was the simple gift that he always cherished, his children and grandchildren. Afterwards, wrapped up in his red Maasai *shuka*, he stood at the porch of the house saying goodbye to his family and waving at them as they drove off in that cold July air.

On Saturday morning, Rev. Jay and his wife left for the hospital in order to have the doctor examine him to find out why the symptoms, which would normally be easily attributed to fatigue, persisted even after he had taken time to rest after the retreat at the Coast. They hadn't told their children that they would be going for the check up. Magadalina Karo did

---

5   A Maasai "shuka" is a blanket-like shawl often with bright
     red and black colours stripes or red and blue colours
     stripes especially wore by the Maasai and Samburu
     communities found in Kenya and some parts of Tanzania.

not want to raise any undue alarm until they had information on what exactly was ailing her husband.

The doctor checked Jay's vital organs and asked him questions mainly on how he was feeling.

"Doctor, Jay has been urinating quite frequently, especially at night," Magadalina volunteered.

"Really," the doctor prodded the couple on.

"Actually doctor, I have been having some burning sensation as well and difficulty in holding back urine. However, it is not until I saw some blood spots in my urine during the last two days that I decided that I should come for a thorough check-up," Rev. Jay said slowly.

The doctor's brow creased but not wanting to send the Karos to a panic, he requested that they return to the hospital the following afternoon for test results. They left the hospital and went on to their favourite restaurant, a few blocks away where Magadalina ordered Rev. Jay's favourite meal. This restaurant held many dear memories for the couple and since she felt a nagging sense of foreboding in her gut, she wanted to have a meal there and add to her list of memories before receiving the test results from the hospital the following day.

The waiters and staff welcomed them as if they were family and soon hot, spicy chicken soup with French beans, Rev. Jay's favourite appetiser, was served. They settled down to the main course in the menu. An elderly couple walked in, the woman especially looked beaten in comparison to the man, like she had recovered from something. As the couple moved to occupy their designated table, the woman's face lit up suddenly, making her appear years younger.

"Jay Karo!" she said out loud. Rev. Jay and Magadalina looked up in their direction and returned the beaming smiles from the couple.

"Mary Karani!" Rev. Jay called back. The two were old time friends who had been in college together. Mary Karani and her husband were Tanzanians but had settled in Kenya and taught at a theological college. After exchanging hearty greetings, they requested to move to another table where they sat and shared with the Tanzanian couple. As they had lunch together and shared about their lives and their children, Rev. Jay and Magadalina learnt that their friend Mary had suffered a stroke and had only recently returned to her normal self. They continued with their conversations late into the afternoon as they had desert and coffee. Before parting ways, they prayed together.

It was 2pm the next day when Magadalina Karo and her husband went back to the hospital for the results of the tests. The doctor greeted them warmly and paced around the office as they settled on the chair. Eventually, he sat down looking down at the report. Suddenly he put on a worried facial expression as he spoke to the couple who he had known for almost twenty years. Holding out the x-ray report, he showed Jay how his prostate gland had enlarged and explained that that was the cause of the problems he has been having with his urinary system. "Jay, we had to conduct some tests on the samples we took from your prostate and I am sorry to tell you that you have a tumour that is malignant, it is cancerous and at an advanced stage!" Magadalina let out a deep sigh and Rev. Jay's chest contracted as he took the news in.

"Doctor what do you suppose we should do? Is there any hope?"

"We will do our best Magadalina, and Jay will have to not only go through surgery but chemotherapy as well and then we will see. We can only do our part and let nature and the Almighty determine how he will recover." the doctor said.

Magadalina was suddenly sinking into a state of anguish and helplessness when she remembered that they were not alone. There had always been a well of hope in her life, which kept her strong in the worst of times. It was the hope she had in God that had proved worthwhile over the years. She remembered a miscarriage she had had at the beginning of her marriage and the delayed conception afterwards. She remembered the tragic loss of her own father when she was still in primary school and how her mother had managed to bring them up into excellent individuals even as a single woman in an era dominated by male cultural oppression which widows underwent.

Magadalina remembered that she had eventually borne four children who had grown up to make them proud. She recalled the road accident that their son Noel had just after joining a national high school and how he had recovered miraculously. She remembered other members of their congregation and friends too who had found God's help in their time of need. *Why, our entire lives have been based on the hope in a living God and his infinite wisdom. This is the school of life we have been to, it is our Alma Mater*, she thought. And yet even with this realisation that strengthened her, she knew that the outlook was grim. Rev. Jay was seventy-five years old and he especially didn't like going to the hospital for the purpose of seeing a doctor. He would easily go and pray for patients, even those whose conditions were hopeless, many of whom recovered. However, it would take all the effort he had when it was his turn to undergo a check up or visit the doctor for whatever ailment.

"I am afraid we have to get Rev. Karo admitted right away Magadalina, unless you have any objection," the doctor said.

Magadalina gave another sigh and with determination, she gave the consent to have Rev. Jay admitted. Before filling in the required paperwork, she called her sons, Noel and Chris, and informed them of what had happened asking them to make their way to the hospital as soon as they could.

Half an hour later, Chris and his wife arrived promptly after an hour, Noel too arrived. Rev. Jay was already admitted and they sat with the doctor who, again, explained to the family about prostate cancer and their father's present state.

They went for a light lunch at the hospital cafeteria although none of them had any appetite. They wanted to leave the hospital with some news that the first stage, which was the operation, had been smooth. After hours, they were called to the doctor's office where they were informed that the operation had been successful but none of them would be allowed to see Rev. Jay since he was still heavily sedated.

Magadalina requested Chris to drive their car as she hardly had the strength to drive herself home. Magadalina Chris' wife drove their own car. They rode home in silence except for the Christian FM radio station playing in the background. They trooped into their parents' home and prayed with their mother before leaving for their own homes, promising to pick her up in the morning so that together they could return to the hospital and attend to their father.

*****

The machine indicating the heartbeat suddenly showed a straight line and a continuous flat sound followed. The doctor moved swiftly, attempting to resuscitate the patient. Several times the shock waves went through Rev. Jay's body; several times Magadalina's heart skipped a beat. However, it was to no avail. Magadalina's lips were dry and though her mind told her that she should say a prayer to reverse what was going on, she was without strength to say it audibly and so she said it in her heart. *Oh God, please don't let Jay die, I still need him.* She was the only one who had been allowed in to see Rev. Jay who was now in the intensive care unit.

Chris, Noel and Sherry heard the sound of a woman crying, and for a moment their minds were unable to assimilate the implication. As they sat there troubled, Chris suddenly got up from his seat as the doctor emerged from the direction of the intensive care unit and walked towards them. Putting on a sombre expression, he broke the news to them.

"I'm afraid your father is in a better place, we tried our best," he said.

Sherry collapsed on her seat in disbelief. "Can we see him?" she asked.

"Yes go ahead before they move the body to the morgue section," he said.

Magadalina's mind went blank and a wave of darkness crossed her view. Her sons stood beside her; Chris holding her. "It is well," he muttered. Elder Andrea walked into the room and with one look at the scene; he understood what was happening.

"I am so sorry," Andrea said hugging Noel, his mother and the rest of the family. Later, other medical personnel walked in, they covered the body and took it away to the morgue.

****

Six days later, a similar crowd to that which had gathered for Noel Karo's ordination, comprising of many more people gathered at Woodlands City Congregation for Rev. Jay Karo's funeral service. Magadalina Karo stood, flanked by both her sons. Her daughters sat next to their brothers. Magadalina was wearing a beautiful black dress and a hat. She didn't wear jewellery or any embellishment, making her look quite plain in comparison to her usual self. Her grandson John walked to where Noel was seated and sat next to his grandmother. There were wreaths which were cream in colour. They would fly the body, along with the family, to Rev. Jay Karo's ancestral home in Kilifi at the coast. Many had booked the night bus to Mombasa to go and attend the funeral which would be held on the next day.

Early on the day of burial, Rev. Jay's father, Mwalimu Karo, sat at the gate and refused to get into the compound until his son's body arrived for burial. Those who had travelled by bus had already begun arriving at the homestead and at about 9:30am a convoy of cars appeared in the distance. Those around Mwalimu Karo informed him that the hearse containing Jay's body as well as the vehicles carrying his family members and close friends had arrived.

Mwalimu Karo looked forlorn and disconsolate, standing at the entrance of the homestead when the convoy arrived. His ashen face made him look older than ever before as tears fell down his cheeks. The drummers had begun beating on their drums and the percussionists played *kayambas*. The notes from several traditional flutes interweaved with other notes into the air rising into a familiar coastal sound, a spectacle for those unfamiliar with the culture, especially those who had come to attend the funeral from other countries. As the cortege arrived and the body was laid in state, there arose the sound of a wonderful hymn Rock of Ages Cleft for Me"[6] 6rendered in pure Swahili. The village women were present as well, clad in bright coloured *lessos*.[7]

The family got out and went to greet Mwalimu Karo and walk him to where the tents had been set up in preparation for the funeral service. Later, May and Sarah, who had flown in, hugged their grandfather. Chris sat with Sarah's husband who was quite unfamiliar with the setting. Noel held Mwalimu Karo's hand as they walked to where they would sit as other guests also stretched to say hello to the late Rev. Jay Karo's wizened father. Mwalimu Karo in turn obliged them and returned as many handshakes as was in his ability to do so until his grandson Noel ushered him to his seat. Soon the service began. There was a little chapel in the heart of this village started by the Baptist church which ran a school as well. Rev. Jay Karo had preached in this little chapel before and recently Noel Karo had done so as well. The Woodlands City Congregation sent donations every so often to the church and school. The pastor in charge of the chapel conducted the service which went on for about two hours. The theme verse was Rev. Jay's favourite verse in his latter days. It was from Psalms 71:18 *"Even when I am old and gray, do not forsake me, O God, till I declare your power to the next generation, your might to all who are to come."*

---

6   "Mwamba wenye Imara" is a Swahili hymn for
     "Rock of Ages Cleft for Me" Full lyrics for "Rock
     of Ages Cleft for Me" at the back of the book.
7   Lessos –a large piece of light cloth with designs printed on
     it and worn by women around the waist and legs or over
     the head and shoulders, especially in East Africa (Swahili).

Several people wanted an early end to the service in order to travel back to their countries and others to Nairobi and to different parts of the country. The pall-bearers included his two sons and elders including Andrea, Galgalo from North Eastern, and Karani whom he had met and had lunch with shortly before his operation. As Mwalimu Karo looked at his grandsons Chris and Noel, his granddaughters and their families, he was consoled knowing that though his son Jay was gone, still there was continuity of his family. He thought of the promises of Psalms 112, especially Psalms 112:2 *"His children will be mighty in the land; the generation of the upright will be blessed."*

At 12pm, the choir and funeral procession moved the body further into a grove of palm trees where they laid the body to rest. The choir voices were raised in the hymn *We're Marching to Zion*[8] this time in English so that the guests could participate. Magadalina Karo's tears now flowed freely as she threw a bunch of earth onto the grave as her children and grandchildren followed. Chris' children who were in their teens were allowed to do so as well as his elder sister Neema's children, the oldest of whom was already 20 years of age and others who were in their late teens. Magadalina Karo had chosen cream flowers for the wreaths and allowed anybody who desired to lay flowers on Rev. Jay's grave to do so in whatever colour they chose. The family laid their wreaths in plenty on the grave and for a moment it was a carpet of cream flowers. The other visitors consisting of friends, colleagues and relatives also added their wreaths on the grave in a multiplicity of colours.

Lunch was served thereafter and most of the guests had lunch as well as the attending villagers. Some guests hurriedly

8   Full hymn at the back

gave their condolences and left. Magadalina Karo, Mwalimu Karo and other family members gathered in their house built next to Mwalimu Karo's little house. Because they had all settled in Nairobi and abroad except for Neema, the house was mostly uninhabited .They ate together and later, most of those who needed to travel back to their various residences left. Only a handful of relatives and a few friends remained. Sheba and Eric Mureithi, Georgina Mumbai and Eusebia were left behind to spend one more night with the family as well. Natasha More and her father-in-law, Jabali More, stayed on too. Jabali More who had grown up alongside Rev. Jay made himself at home. However, his son Samba More had to leave for some urgent business. Michael Mumbai, Georgina's husband, had travelled out of the country. In her characteristic way, Eusebia had already joined in the chores of the homestead, especially helping to attend to the needs of Magadalina Karo and her immediate family.

The Giriama[9] village elders came to pay their respects to Magadalina Karo and the rest of the family, including Rev. Jay's siblings and their children who were at the funeral. It was the tradition in the community, to let the local liquor known as *Mnazi*[10] flow freely during funerals and celebrations. On this occasion however, Magadalina Karo would obviously not allow anything of the sort since theirs was a Christian family keen on being a good example and following Christian teachings. Jabali[11] More had insisted on paying for the food catered at the funeral and had later on decided to buy a hundred crates of soda to compensate for the lack of liquor so that the villagers

9   A Kenyan coastal sub-tribe which is part of
      the larger tribe known as Mijikenda.
10   Palm wine.
11   Rock.

would not feel like the Karo's were being snobbish and so the villagers drank soda almost uncontrollably. The Karos didn't try to stop them or Jabali More and his gestures of solidarity. They were sure Rev. Jay himself would not have stopped them either. Jabali More was a widower himself, who had recently entertained a woman for a period of time - about three years - only to have later decided that she was a waste of time; more of a trophy and would never fit into a wife's shoes.

At 7pm the weather suddenly changed and it began raining, sending the younger of the villagers who were still enjoying drinks scattering to their various homesteads as heavy rain drops poured endlessly until it was raining cats and dogs. "It has been so long since it last rained. Rev. Jay Karo was a good man," one of the Giriama elders stated. Jabali sat with the elders under a *makuti*[12] shelter in the compound till late in the night. Early the next morning, at 8am, he bid Magadalina Karo and her family farewell and left for the airport to catch the 10am flight.

---

12   Dry palm fronds referred to as 'makuti' when used for roofing and as temporary shelters.

Chapter 3

When Noel put forward his plan for a new church auditorium to the board, it was received with much enthusiasm. Lately, Noel had demonstrated that he was a man of vision and not simply his father's protégé. Pastor Seth, who had been the associate Pastor and next in rank to Rev. Jay Karo, had supported Noel. Rev Jay had appointed Pastor Seth who was about sixty years of age, to an advisory role in the other two congregations and projects spread across the country even as he remained in active service as associate Pastor in the capital. However, Noel Karo, his son who had served in the church as a pastor for about three years would be the visionary Pastor and leader in charge of this particular congregation.

After Rev. Jay's death, most authority had shifted to his younger son, and with it some discomfort. It was emerging that Pastor Seth would have preferred the leading role in this main congregation instead of retaining his position as associate Pastor and having an overall advisory role at Woodlands City Congregation as well as the other two congregations which were much smaller. Some of those who dearly loved him - as followers usually grow to dearly love their leaders - also felt that perhaps it would have been a better decision to have Pastor Seth take over as the lead pastor of Woodlands City Congregation. Nevertheless, it was increasingly evident that Pastor Noel Karo was a leader who stood on his own as well.

Pastor Noel Karo worked easily with the other members of the pastoral team. He loved many aspects of being a pastor. He had begun witnessing first hand change in people's lives. People might come into a service altogether indifferent or weighed down by life and in a few weeks, tangible change could be viewed in their state of mind, if not in the circumstances they were facing. He had learnt to take the dark moments too when he had to conduct a funeral or when there were those ailing in hospital or members facing marital hardships brought about by a myriad of factors. Recently, he had referred an older couple who had been married for thirty years with a counselling issue to Pastor Seth and a Christian psychologist who was a member of the church.

He felt disturbed though that only a fraction of the members turned up when the tasks perceived as less interesting needed to be carried out. In a congregation consisting of three thousand, only a handful, about 200 members, usually turned up for the weekly prayer meeting. The situation would be worse when it came to a combined period of prayer and fasting.

He was however thankful that the members were altogether enthusiastic about coming to church and giving. They hardly ran out of funds. This enabled them to concentrate on the core work which is to grow and nurture a congregation into Christian maturity and to impact the surrounding world with the gospel. There were those members who were loyal and always stood by the leadership all year round. There were those who attended regularly, but mostly at their convenience. There were those who attended by virtue of a committed family member, especially the children of those members who had joined the church in the initial years when his father, Rev. Jay Karo, had began his calling. A few of these were Noel's age group and older. Some of their children were already young adults. Noel's children, John and Miriam, were now ten and thirteen years respectively. In ten years or more, these would be married with offspring. The changing demographics of the country and the church had informed the decision Rev. Jay Karo had made to appoint his own son as the lead Pastor. The population was increasingly youthful and the church was following suit and therefore in need of youthful visionary leadership alongside the older leadership. Pastor Noel had been in his care since his childhood and though he was only thirty-five years old, he had been exposed to this kind of environment all his life. More than half of the board of elders had endorsed his decision. *With God's help, it would be difficult to fail*, Rev. Jay had concluded.

*****

As Pastor Noel entered the boardroom he was greeted by inquiring eyes. He smiled uneasily across the room, surprised that everyone was already seated about five minutes to the time the meeting was to commence. Usually, the earliest to arrive would come in at the exact hour, 10am. The atmosphere felt a little charged and for some reason he felt a little uncomfortable, even apprehensive.

He didn't have his father, the late Rev. Jay, with him, but he trusted that God was on his side. Lately, his father's dear friend, elder Andrea and three other board members were the only ones who had tried to understand him and the only ones who stood by him even as he faltered in his bigger mistakes as a leader. The church members had received the plans for expansion proposed by the leadership with much joy but the reality of continually making contributions towards the project in the face of a dwindling economy seemed too hard to bear.

Many felt that Pastor Noel Karo, in his ambition to do something worthwhile for God, had become somewhat insensitive to the prevailing economic climate. It was now two years since he had prevailed upon the board of elders to suspend their annual tradition of contributing towards the needs of the elderly and poor as a church, at least until they completed their current project. As part of their outreach programme, his father, the late Rev. Jay, had left a legacy of caring for the poor in different places within the country. This had been in addition to caring for those in their immediate environment with similar needs. An amount of money would be allocated to this extra cause within the annual church budget. It was initially three million shillings but had grown into five million shillings just before the passing on of Rev. Jay Karo.

Due to the magnificent church auditorium to be built, the offering was collected about three times on Sunday and once during the two midweek services they held. Noel had noticed that the finances collected at the church had slightly decreased. It was not difficult to pinpoint some factors that had led to the decrease, as he was aware that at least thirty faithful members of the congregation had been retrenched as some multinationals downsized their staff in the country. These were among the loyal and regular members of the church. Some members' businesses were making losses due to various factors. It was expensive to do business the straight and narrow way, especially for those who import products. Though they had the means, they would encounter delays in clearing their goods, since they wouldn't bribe their way through the customs officials so that their goods are cleared in time. These delays had implications on the profit margin.

After a word of prayer, one of the elders spoke, "We are glad that you have vision concerning the direction this congregation should be taking, especially in improving capacity, and in this respect, building the new church sanctuary. However, as we have noticed in the tithes and offerings, members are experiencing difficult financial times and some are losing their jobs or livelihoods. Don't you think we should slow down on the building and collections? Noel no doubt, you are a gifted leader who loves God but experience is just as useful and perhaps for some time someone with greater experience should be at the helm, just for a time. Elders, we are suggesting that you let Pastor Seth take over the position of senior pastor and lead the way for some time and after about ten years or less, you will be in a better position to be the senior pastor."

Pastor Noel Karo's mind flashed back to the board's activities over the last few weeks. Before coming to a decision, they had so far always discussed and the majority had usually prevailed except in cases when it was the sole prerogative of the pastor to decide on a certain issue. Pastor Seth and part of the elders had once suggested taking a loan in order to boost the building fund and therefore avoid taking slow steps which may in the end affect the quality of the building altogether. However, Pastor Noel Karo and another section of elders had decided against taking that direction. The congregation gave steadily, they had argued, and further, they felt that it wouldn't be right for the money collected from members to be used to pay off interest on a loan in the future. They argued that, in the Bible, providence was always made when God initiated a particular work.

*****

It was increasingly becoming difficult for Pastor Noel to make quick decisions concerning the church with the help of the elders and deacons. Whenever a decision needed to be made, there was a section of the board of elders who always had a contrary opinion to the direction Pastor Noel wanted to take even when their difference in opinion was openly unjustifiable. This section of elders was the one which had suggested that Pastor Seth takes over as senior pastor for a while.

Unknown to Pastor Noel, Pastor Seth and his close supporters had gathered part of the congregation who felt that indeed the older pastor should have been given the lead responsibility in the church. Urged on by some congregants as well as a wounded ego, he had decided to break away and had rented a hall where he would conduct church services. It was true that Pastor Seth had worked alongside the late Rev. Jay Karo for many years and he had prospered too in what they had accomplished together as well as with others. However, he found it difficult to stop feeling offended that Rev. Jay Karo had elected to choose his son Noel as the next leader, especially after Rev. Jay's death. And then the worst had happened. One Sunday about half of the congregation went missing. In a single day, Pastor Noel Karo had seen slightly over one thousand members of his congregation leave the church. Though those left were happy to be at church, Pastor Noel had no idea why so many members were missing. It took a meeting with Elder Andrea and another pastor that afternoon, to gently break the news to him. Elder Andrea had got wind of the breakaway earlier that month but since he had no evidence on it, he had hesitated to tell Pastor Noel about it. Instead, he had spoken to a few other members who went into prayer about the whole issue. Elder Andrea had resolved to wait and see how many people would leave in order to advise Pastor Noel on the way forward.

How is it that he had failed to contain the ominous threat of discord, disunity, division and disharmony? Pastor Noel Karo wondered. In the following month after the church split, Pastor Noel Karo had been disconsolate. It had been an extremely difficult period, as much as Elder Andrea, his wife Sherry, and the remaining leadership and congregation tried to encourage him. For a whole week, Elder Andrea had taken over the role of speaking to disquieted church members and the other pastoral staff had handled the services. Pastor Noel didn't report to work at the church office for the whole week. On that Friday evening, Elder Andrea and few other remaining members of the elders and deacon board went to visit him at his residence and encouraged him. Elder Andrea had bought a couple of books with recorded experiences of other church ministers who had encountered various trials and failures along the way, but had triumphed. However, Pastor Noel Karo didn't manage to run a single church service for that entire month and would fail to report to his office on certain days of the week.

A month later, he began reading the books gifted to him and he felt much better. He remembered that his late father was a man of courage, always. Rev. Jay Karo had endured much over the years. When he made mistakes, he had suffered but nevertheless, he hadn't given up. Pastor Noel Karo resolved to get up and go on with the journey.

He resumed his pastoral duties and encouraged the remaining members of the congregation. With the departure of such a large number of members, nagging thoughts of failure haunted Pastor Noel from time to time but he brushed them off with courage, speaking verses of help and encouragement to himself from the Bible. In a few weeks, they would carry out an analysis of what had led to the church split and where things might be done better in the future. As painful as it may be, he wanted to own his part in the situation they had found themselves in.

*****

It was an early morning in July when Pastor Noel hurried to work in order to continue with his tasks for that particular day. Earlier on he had been at the church compound to conduct morning prayers with a few members. As he entered the lobby, he was met by a group of ten individuals, both men and women. From their clothing, he could tell that they had travelled a long distance. Their clothing was a little crumpled and dusty as well. Nevertheless, they were quietly seated in the lobby. An elderly man's face – about sixty - lit up when he saw Pastor Noel Karo walk in.

"Pastor Noel, hello!" he cried.

Suddenly, Pastor Noel realised that this was actually Elder Galgalo from Northern Kenya and his mind quickly bounced to the present. He looked at the gathering, and a smile came on his face as he began to greet each one of them heartily. These were representatives of the mission projects they supported in remote areas of the northern, coastal and western parts of the country. Their faces were haggard and some of them appeared to have been dozing before he came into the reception. "When did you arrive?" he asked Galgalo.

"We arrived yesterday at about 5:30 pm in the evening but we could not find you on phone and we rang the church office

35

but there was no one to pick up the call since we had arrived late."

"Where did you spend the night then?" he asked.

"We hired a room in town where at least each of us could sit and doze a little and perhaps wash our faces before coming here this morning," he answered. Galgalo's wife sat next to him. Pastor Noel looked at the lot and made a decision that they should rest and have a meal before he attended to them.

He entered his office and called his wife, explaining the situation.

"Please have the visitors dropped here at home and I will make sure that they take a shower and have something to eat and rest until the evening when you come," Sherry suggested.

"My thoughts exactly," Pastor Noel answered.

He then called in the church secretary and instructed her to have the driver drop the group at their house. He returned to the lobby and explained to them that he would have to meet them in the evening and then listen to what they had to say. Sherry called her friend, George Mumbai, who came in with her ever helpful house help, Eusebia. With Sherry and George's supervision, Sherry's domestic worker, a cook known as Tom and Eusebia got breakfast ready.

Sherry was delighted to have the visitors join her for the day. She quickly showed them into the dining room where breakfast had been prepared. The women had decided to take a bath first and thereafter, they joined the men for breakfast. They had tea, eggs, sausages, bread and fruit. Some took porridge. Later the men were lead to the guest wing where they could take a shower. The guest wing was divided into two wings with twin beds in each, a shower room and a toilet. The ladies used one wing while the six men used the other.

As the men went to take a shower, the women chatted on with Sherry and George, speaking of the weather back at their areas, their homes, their children, the church congregations and general happenings. Later, they narrated some difficulties they were facing. In about an hour's time, the men had joined them and they narrated various stories of triumph and loss at their work. Before they knew it, it was already 1:30pm and they were invited to the dining room for lunch. Sherry and George had made grilled chicken, fried rice, *chapati* and salad. There were all kinds of soda as well.

At 3pm, the guests trooped away to the guest wing to take a nap. Sherry made arrangements for dinner as they rested. At exactly 5pm Pastor Noel had returned from work. After exchanging greetings, George excused herself, leaving with Eusebia. "That was time well spent," she said and gave Sherry a hug.

"Thank you, see you soon!" Sherry answered, walking her to where she had parked her car. The exhausted guests were still fast asleep. They came out of their rooms at 7pm. Soon, a cup of tea was served.

"How has your day been?" Pastor Noel asked them. "Are you feeling any better?"

"We are feeling much better," Galgalo replied. "You have treated us like kings and we thank you very much. You are truly Jay's son. May God bless you! However, Pastor Noel, my son, we would like to let you know why we have travelled this far."

"I understand, Elder Galgalo. Please let us know everything." he said.

Elder Galgalo then set to articulate the condition of the various projects that the Woodlands Congregation Church had been supporting. Before they decided to take a short break and concentrate on the church building project, they had given about five million shillings annually, which was divided amongst the four mission fields. However, because of the building project, they had been unable to do so for the last two years. Initially, Noel had intended to skip the support for only one year but after that year had come to an end, the project was still at its crucial stages and the finances had started reducing. They were now at the threshold of a new year and at their lowest point, financially. From Elder Galgalo's speech, Noel realised that a lot of children had suffered worse nutrition due to lack in the feeding programme and other members of the community as well due to lack of medicine in the mission dispensary. Similarly, a well that had been long planned for had not been drilled due to lack of funds.

"The support Woodlands City Congregation has been giving us is very crucial Pastor Noel. It greatly supplements the other efforts on the ground. We do not ask that you give us five million shillings at once but that you would consider even half the amount in your budget this year, to alleviate the condition we are in," Elder Masinde pleaded.

"The church board, the pastoral team and I will look into this issue, the soonest we can," Pastor Noel intimated. "Meanwhile, I have booked your return tickets and I thank you for coming."

Sherry had packed some good clothing that the children had overgrown. She handed this to the women. Dinner was served at 9pm and they ate quietly, holding light conversation. The guests were all grateful for the hospitality they had encountered at Pastor Noel Karo's house. They decided to hold a session of joint prayer and present all their requests to God. It was a little after midnight when they retreated to sleep. By 6am, the guests were all awake, making preparations to leave, and at 8am they had breakfast together.

"You know what elders, we are going to work on a plan to not only support you in ministry but to help your community get more empowered and to hopefully graduate to a place where you no longer need to rely on us as such, you know," Sherry Karo stated and Pastor Noel Karo repeated the same to them in flawless coastal Kiswahili. The guests were shuttled to their various bus stations to make the journey back to their homes.

Pastor Noel tossed and turned the entire night. He had slowly become less aware of how much their contribution as a church had helped to build other people's lives and had instead laid quite some emphasis on the building project.

Lately, Mwalimu Karo, also known as "Papa" was getting sickly more often and Pastor Noel decided to visit him and spend time with him since he was his only living grandparent. Mwalimu Karo had grieved deeply when his son Rev. Jay had passed on. Nevertheless, he understood that what Jay had been preaching all the while had now come to pass - that *"to be absent in the body is to be present with the Lord"* (2Cor.5:8). His father had always given him words of wisdom when he needed them and now maybe Papa would do the same.

Chapter 4

He took a day bus to Mombasa and then to Kilifi, his father's ancestral home and where his grandfather still lived. The land between Nairobi and Mombasa was mainly uninhabited with some scrubland and savannah. A large part consisted of the great Tsavo East and Tsavo West national parks. This particular aspect especially made an impression on him at this time, a suitable metaphor of how his life was currently stuck in a barren stretch. His life felt like scrubland and savannah. It was a long drive with time to take lunch at Mtito Andei which was half the journey, 440km away from Nairobi. It was always a heart-warming relief when there was the final drastic change in temperatures and the sight of palm trees waving their fronds in the wind. Here, everybody usually took off their jackets and sweaters, in obedience to the coastal weather. Most of the people disembarked at Mombasa and then the bus continued on its way to Kilifi. It had been a long time since Pastor Noel took the journey by road in a public bus and it was a breathtaking sight to him as he looked at the land stretching out to the horizon. A large part of it before Kilifi town consisted of sisal growing estates. Once in Kilifi, the local Baptist pastor at his father's village was waiting to pick him up and take him to his grandfather's house.

*****

Pastor Noel's heart was always drawn to older people. He loved listening to their stories. It was interesting to note how the world in its rush scarcely noticed them or took them seriously and yet, what the older members of society treasured most were sons, daughters, grandchildren and great grandchildren. As Pastor Noel looked at elderly people who had lived many more years than his own and had somehow triumphed, he knew that he too would triumph. *"I see my eyes in your eyes, Noel, and my face in your face,"* his grandfather would tell him, meaning this as a compliment. *"I was just as energetic and social as you are when I was young,"* he would add.

"Your father was a quiet man, he took after his mother and his balanced nature helped him accomplish much, especially when he had learnt to love people and not fear them. When he had learnt not to think much about how he was regarded by men but rather to pour out himself and be the best," he stated.

Grandpa Mwalimu Karo was simply known as "Papa" in the village. He didn't try to understand everything about the present world but he was keen that his children should understand their times and the value of those things that do not change. It was amazing how much old people valued the company of younger people when they visited them and humoured them.

"When one is young, my grandchild, it is easy to feel love and life from all sources, but in old age, movement is limited and times have changed, many friends have died and it is no longer possible to enjoy what one used to enjoy," Grandpa said slowly.

Noel watched his frail grandfather, now ninety-five years of age. His white hair was much less now than it had been when they had been younger. He served him some soup brought in by Apophia, the village woman who cooked for him and took care of his needs for a monthly wage. Due to his advanced age, he had been a convalescent from time to time and sometimes, his dependency was similar to a baby's. When he would ask for anything to eat, the village woman would bend over backwards to get him what he had asked for even though she may have planned to cook something else. Sometimes he wanted fish which was widely available. Since he couldn't get rid of the fish bones as he ate, Apophia would go into town to look for fish fillet at a certain butchery, the only one selling fish fillet, operated by an Arab family. All of Papa's food was cooked using coconut oil which was very healthy especially now that he was aged. Presently, he was in high spirits despite his increasingly frailty, and Pastor Noel spent many hours conversing under the shade of his favourite palm tree, where a cane chair was permanently placed for him.

Mwalimu Karo liked it when his grandchildren told him stories. They kept him abreast of all the latest happenings; how the world was turning out to be. He liked it specifically when Pastor Noel spoke to him about politics and events around the country.

"We complain of colonialism and white missionaries; their brutality, and how they tried to change us into what we are not. We aren't white after all and will never be, we say. The colonisers disrespected our culture and called it primitive. They viewed themselves as civilising us natives. Yes, almost all that is true and yet with the bad came the good like formal education, better health and agriculture, clothes, easier access to water, electricity and transport among numerous changes that are now evident all over the country. Remote places grew into towns in a few years of colonisation. However, today, almost fifty years after independence, there are places where people remain dirt poor, and far-flung regions where the educated fear to tread lest they be infected with disease; become victims of dreaded witchcraft spells, lose daily access to amenities afforded by the modern life and its comforts or suffer murder due to insecurity. You cannot convince me that there is any race that is purely righteous and devoid of the evils characteristic of mankind. I believe that human beings in the end must be judged on individual basis. A man's actions, omissions and choices define him, no matter what his tribe or race," Mwalimu Karo said.

Pastor Noel wondered if life was judging him by his actions. He had put in all his energy into the church and did all he knew best to nurture the members. How is it that all his effort seemingly resulted in the emptying of pews as the congregation shrunk with every Sunday?

The emptying church auditorium felt strange. In the past year he had maintained a congregation of about 950 members until when the numbers had again shrunk to about 500 members, some of whom had families. Some families remained members of the church but became irregular in attendance; some were his personal friends, like Sheba and Eric whose attendance had become somewhat irregular. George's husband and their house help were also increasingly missing. Salome the widow was altogether missing just as Samba, the parliamentarian. Teresa had disappeared for a month only to return and become as loyal as ever in her service to God and other members besides enrolling for a Bible course.

"Papa I am trying to build God a house, a bigger one that will seat seven thousand people. We have worked together as the church leadership, at least most of the time until things fell apart. It is going to be the most magnificent church auditorium yet, just wait until we finish and ..." Pastor Noel said before getting interrupted by Grandpa.

"And what then?" Grandpa asked. "What is a house anyway? Just a structure," grandfather began. "Just look at your father Jay, he didn't even wear shoes initially when he started going to school. He started school pretty late too, not like my great grandchildren - your children little John and Miriam who were already in school at four years of age. We lived in a mud structure in those days, Noel. My grandson, a voice spoke to my heart in those hard, uncertain days; saying that I, Mwalimu Karo, could indeed have a great house. I followed the pull within my innermost man, my conscience, to follow Christ and his ways even though the White man wasn't always agreeable." He continued reflectively, "I thought, 'If we are children of one father as they claimed though, then maybe our father had sent them to rescue us from a certain form of darkness, and they too would be rescued when they needed it,' I thought. Light shone in my path and I thank God Noel that I began building that house. That house was my children, teaching them to fear God and giving them an education when it wasn't that popular to do so."

Pastor Noel sat still, listening to his grandfather. "Today I live in a real stone house with a servant to take care of me and my children and grandchildren to visit me. My four sons and three daughters all have admirable homes and families of their own. And Jay the pearl in my heart became a pastor and did a great, respectable work of serving God and people. My grandchild, it is good that you want to exceed your father. Better still, it is good that you want to glorify God by building him this wonderful modern house of worship. You have shown me a picture of how it would be when it is finally complete and it is wonderful. Your father Jay didn't manage to build as big an auditorium as you want to but he succeeded in building a larger house. My child, the hearts of poor people in desolate places, without God and without hope have been reached. They have no running water, sometimes starving, without clothes and many times without access to a decent education or a stable church... that is the house Jay was slowly helping to build. Why did you stop the annual contribution to the mission fields my grandson? Do you think God will support your work when you do this kind of thing? A house consists of people and not bricks and mortar. People. You shouldn't give up on the dream to have the house of worship but yet you shouldn't leave the other more important work undone." Mwalimu Karo concluded.

****

Mwalimu Karo sat on his chair under the palm tree and enjoyed conversations with those who came to visit him. There was always a visitor passing by or a villager saying hello or in need of advice. Pastor Noel joined him and in this way he got to interact with the locals. Ignorance and superstition was still rife here and it was mainly due to the slower uptake of education and serious Christianity. At one point Pastor Noel would find himself counselling various young Giriama girls, some of whom had no concrete issue to discuss as such but wanted to speak with him out of curiosity perhaps. It was therefore amusing when his grandfather told him that perhaps some wished he would take them up for a second wife! Noel shook his head at the thought. *Human behaviour cuts across cultures*, he thought. Back at Woodlands City Congregation, there would be the genuine girls and women who required prayer and counsel as well as those who came to his office either out of curiosity and an innocent attraction or for their own ill motives. It was crucial for him to discern motives and to have a code of conduct with those of the female gender. However, he was glad that he had the chance of interacting with the locals and he continually counselled them, enlightening their minds that life had God given choices and possibilities and was not simply fatalism. As he reflected on the conditions of his kinsmen, he knew that it would take tens of years for the spiritual and developmental challenges they faced to be overcome. He hoped that the support they gave to the Baptist mission would count in the uplifting of the community.

During the third week of his visit, Noel went on a 7-day fast where he took fluids only in order to avoid dehydration. It was a difficult time to both his body and his mind but he had to remember that his spirit was being strengthened and that he would find hope and direction for the journey.

*****

Pastor Noel looked at the picture of his late father as he took his cup of tea. His grandfather's advice was sound. It was hard to believe that Mwalimu was ninety-five years old at this time and that his memory failed him sometimes. The next few years were going to be difficult for him but he would have to bear it. If ever he had believed that there is life after death, he believed it now more than ever. He would do his best to make his father Jay proud up there in heaven. However, the reality of a dilapidating building project and its equivalent shame was beginning to take a toll on him. Pastor Noel decided to dispose of his two cars which had cost about three million shillings collectively, being relatively new as well as his home built on half an acre of land which was worth about twelve million shillings with its surrounding compound. He planned to keep one car and move into a smaller, old apartment owned by his parents and which was currently being let out for rent. For this, he needed his mother's permission. He had made calculations that showed that the remainder of the building project required about twenty million shillings to bring it to a level of basic maintenance without any work having been done on the interiors. After that it would require forty million Kenya shillings more to be complete with all the facilities. Its interiors could be enhanced later. If he successfully managed to sell these two items, he would have raised a good amount. It would also be much easier on his conscience, considering his past mistakes. He needed to speak to his wife Sherry, Andrea, the chairman of the board of elders and deacons, his mother and his elder brother to inform them of his decision.

Chapter 5

With the turning tide of life, Sherry had found herself with less work to do concerning the church and therefore more time in her hands. She became keener in pursuing her art. She was comforted by the control that an artist has over their artwork. Unlike their present life circumstances, with her paint and brush, she was at least sure of one outcome in her life: the outcome of her creativity would be as she desired, most of the time.

Pastor Noel had retreated to his grandfather's place. He said he would be away for a month. It was important for him to spend time with his grandfather, especially then, he said, since he could pass away at any time.

Suddenly, the house seems quite empty. Noel's presence greatly warms this house, for sure, Sherry thought. With the children away in school at daytime, she knew there was a chance to incorporate something extra into her schedule. Lately, Sherry had been thinking of holding an art exhibition and to invite both local and international guest artists to participate. Through participating in exhibitions, she had met and made a few friends internationally. The exhibition would rally around specific themes. At the top of her head she had the themes of *Surrender vs. Indifference, Freewill* and yet another one

Universal Man. Each artist would paint along the same themes and this way there would be a variety of artistic interpretations around a similar theme. She decided to involve five other artists, one from Kenya, a gentleman known as Kipyegon who was a fellow artist and dear friend, two from the United States, one from India and another one from South Africa.

The money collected would be used to raise funds for the church auditorium. The artists would also participate in contributing to the decor aspects of the church auditorium. Sherry began making phone calls. She began by phoning Jerome Nicholas and Martha Ferguson who were both in the United States and with whom she had shared a class with during her earlier college days. However, the two were now living in different States. Catching them on their home numbers took a number of days due to the difference in time zones both within the States and in comparison to Kenya. However, towards the end of the week, she received a phone call from Jerome and Martha. They were both enthusiastic about the idea of doing a work of art for a good purpose. They were both born again Christians who had committed their lives to God during their college years.

Meanwhile, Sherry had begun buying material to use for her paintings. Canvas, pencils, oil paints and everything else she needed to get her project started. She had began with prayer and meditation the moment the idea came to mind and already she had inspiration for one or two pieces for the exhibition. Her first piece was titled *Indifference*.

I should consider the state of the world and its peoples. Most people acknowledge that it is difficult to live life on one's own effort and therefore acknowledge their need for a higher power. Many times people are exposed to the knowledge of God through the Bible and God's love for mankind. However, it is a great irony that when it comes to responding to the offer of salvation given through the suffering for sin on the cross, a needy world turns its back on the only true hope, not necessarily out of hate for God but a gigantic, stubborn looming indifference, she thought.

After consulting with her husband, Pastor Noel, Sherry had decided to hold the exhibition on the last week of November in the next year. This would be ideal as usually, most people are already in a holiday mood during this month as the Christmas season approaches. This would afford maximum traffic to the exhibition and hopefully, art lovers would be in a disposition to spend more at this time.

Sherry had already mounted her canvas for the centrepiece of her collection. She had made the sketches and slowly the painting had begun to take shape. The painting consisted of different people whose arms were interlocked and they formed a ring or circle. They were both native peoples of various continents and modern people dressed in everyday clothing. The garb adorned by the various types of peoples was itself spectacular, as well as their features. The people had their backs to a very strong white light in the centre of the circle facing the outside. The outside however was dark, beginning with a slight shadow from where they stood going on to a stronger darkness and finally pitch darkness at the further end of the painting. This was Sherry's centrepiece, *Indifference*. Meanwhile Martha Ferguson and Jerome Nicholas were getting ready with their own paintings.

Pastor Noel was due to arrive from his retreat at his grandfather's place. They had spoken on phone about the whole idea of the art exhibition, and Sherry had also visited him on one weekend at their father's home and spent some time together. However, she would take comfort when he came home and together, they critiqued the work that she had done so far. Pastor Noel appreciated art and his wife's artistic abilities. He was both a valued fan and critic to her.

He arrived at the close of the week, as Sherry was baking in the kitchen with Tom, the cook. As Noel drove into the compound, Sherry hurried to the front door and the parking and welcomed him home. He looked darker, probably a tan from the sun obtained from spending some time outdoors with nature and his grandfather. He looked healthier as well, perhaps from sharing the very healthy diet his grandfather ate. *We will borrow a leaf from grandpa's diet* Sherry said to herself and made a mental note to carry it through.

Pastor Noel in turn looked at his wife, surprisingly, very glad to be back home. He had really missed her. *I wonder if Sherry will assent to my decision to sell this lovely home*, he thought. They walked on to the house and as dusk approached, the cook and the house help retreated to their quarters. Pastor Noel narrated to his wife how spending time with his grandfather had been. It had been three weeks of quietness and he had had time to think and pray about what lay ahead. He had also had the privilege of enjoying his grandfather's wise counsel.

Sherry prepared a pot of coffee and served Pastor Noel and herself some as well as a slice of the cake she had baked previously. They sat inside her painting studio that also doubled as the music room and conversed. He was awed at the metaphor that the painting *Indifference* was but nevertheless, he had a few suggestions on how to improve it.

Making a change in the conversation they were having, he shared with his wife his thoughts about selling their home and their two cars. He did not put his decision forward as final but asked for her consent and support.

"Honey, if you feel we shouldn't then I won't sell our home. We can sell the two cars and leave the house." Pastor Noel looked at Sherry, her eyes were as wide as saucers and he could see bewilderment, fear and uncertainty in her eyes. He knew that this would be hard on Sherry. He had promised to take care of her and to the best of his ability afford her a good life, similar to that which she would have had in America right here in Kenya at least as much as it would be in his power to do so. Sherry's heart sank. It was hard to think of having to leave their home with its beautiful design and surrounding gardens. Nevertheless, their economic condition was dire and the church building was at risk of lying dilapidated and being a cause for shame. Besides, ultimately, they were God's servants and if he had given them this house in the first instance, he would do it again. He would give them another home eventually. They went to sleep in contemplation.

In the morning Sherry woke up to an early telephone call from her friend Jerome Nicholas, who told her that he had sent her a scanned image of his first painting whose theme and title was *Freewill*.

"Brace yourself for it may surprise you," he said. Sherry got up and brewed a cup of coffee. She quickly sat at the computer and accessed her email. "It's the best thing that ever happened in governance this side of heaven, the closest political system in tandem with the aspect of Freewill," Jerome had said.

His painting though just a scan looked magnificent. The canvas had been split into two by a blue sky and it was clear that below the blue sky was earth and above the blue sky was heaven. *The painting has a wonderful three dimensional effect to it*, Sherry thought. The people in heaven had freely chosen to follow God and his rule and the people on earth in a democratic government had also chosen whatever direction they wanted to follow, whether good or bad. Sherry mused at Jerome's painting and perspective as she went on to take a shower. Pastor Noel who had woken up earlier and gone to pray came into the bedroom just as she stepped out of the shower.

During breakfast, Sherry spoke, "Maybe it is time to show our devotion to our call and the work of Christ. Since he has sacrificed for us, then we too can sacrifice what we have for him," Sherry said. "I will support you in your decision."

Pastor Noel breathed a great sigh of relief. If he had managed to obtain his wife's support, then his mother would give her consent too, at least that's what he would like to think.

He phoned his mother and his brother and requested them for a meeting, the following weekend, at their mother's house. Meanwhile, the progress with the exhibition plan encouraged Sherry to press on. Later in the week Martha Ferguson had sent a scan of her centrepiece, *Universal Man*, through email. The painting was the person of Jesus Christ, with features similar to the famous Da Vinci portrait but yet he was standing tall, dressed in the garments of a Maasai warrior complete with the head decorations, neck beads and sandals. The *shuka* wrapped around him was a glorious red. His eyes were piercing and it looked quite unique that a Caucasian Jesus Christ would be dressed as he was.

Sherry had been working on a surprise portrait and he wanted to show it to Pastor Noel and his family. They would be having dinner at their house on Friday of that particular week. After they had dinner and were relaxing over a cup of coffee,

Sherry invited everyone to the studio. "I have been working on the painting exhibition with my friends Jerome, Martha and Koros whom you all know about," she started. "There is a special painting to me among what we have been doing so far but I wanted you to also take a look and let me know your thoughts about it. The name of this particular painting is *Another Life*."

"Honey, come and help me pull this cover," she requested her husband.

Pastor Noel went over to the painting. "I'll get it," he said gently pulling the covering sheet from the top corners and whisking it off the painting. Suddenly, the studio went quiet.

"Oh!" Magadalina gasped. "It's so beautiful!" "This is wonderful," Chris exclaimed.

There were smiles on faces as well as teary eyes. Magadalina had taken out her handkerchief and was dabbing off teardrops from her eyes. "Thank you for reminding me," she said and gave Sherry a long warm, hug. Pastor Noel kissed his wife and congratulated her and everyone in the studio hugged her and congratulated her as well.

The room was alight with the portrait of Rev. Jay Karo in his latter days, before his health had failed. Sherry had taken one of his best photographs among many others and had painted it into a sizeable portrait. She had used white, gold and blue as the backdrop and the result had been a dazzling light that made Rev. Jay appear to be in a glorious place, what heaven may look like. She had managed to capture both his features and the emotion making the portrait come to life.

As they later sat down to eat, Pastor Noel Karo brought up the topic of their discussion with Sherry on the previous night. "Mother, Chris and everybody, we are planning to sell this house and two of our cars," Noel began. "You know how tough things have been and the sudden reduction of funds coming into the church since there was a split. It is going to be quite shameful for the building project to come to a total halt. As we try to sort out everything else and wait for things to get better, Sherry and I have decided to dispose off some of our assets. This will help to keep the building project going and prevent its laying there dilapidated. I am hoping that you will support us in this decision," he concluded.

Everyone was silent and attentive as he spoke. After a minute or so, Magadalina Karo spoke. "Where do you plan to live after that?" she asked.

"We are seeking your permission to move to the old flat you and father have been renting over the years," he answered. The flat in question had two large bedrooms and was generally spacious. This is where Rev. Jay and Magadalina Karo stayed in their early years of marriage. All their children except the last born had been born while they lived there.

Chris patted Noel on the back. "That's quite a sacrifice, man," he said.

"Why don't you come and live with me instead?" Magadalina asked. "The house is big and without your father Jay, it gets quite lonesome sometimes."

"Oh mother, we wouldn't want to impose," Sherry answered.

"Impose? On the contrary, I could do with some company. And my grandchildren would fill my days with sunshine," Magadalina Karo said almost pleadingly.

"Actually that's an excellent suggestion mother," Chris answered.

"Yeah it's great," May agreed. "I have been with mother for the past couple of months but now I need to go back to the States and I can imagine she will be lonely," she added.

"Sherry, I am going to let you redecorate the house to your liking and I will be at the adjoining guest room. It is quite large and will be sufficient for me," Magadalina insisted.

Sherry was at a loss for words. *Moving into my mother-in-laws house would be an honour and the children's lives would be enriched as they spend time with her*, she thought. She glanced at Pastor Noel approvingly. Pastor Noel hesitated as Sherry fixed her glance on him.

"Are you sure about this mother?" he asked.

"Of course I am," Magadalina replied.

"Okay then, we will move in with you mother," he said and Sherry smiled as Magadalina laughed in delight.

"Thank you so much mother," Sherry and Noel said in unison.

"You're welcome my son, you're welcome my daughter," she replied.

"It's settled then," Chris concluded.

They continued with their dinner and conversation and later left for their homes. A month later, Magadalina moved to the guest wing of her house giving Sherry room to redecorate the house according to her taste. Another month passed and Sherry and Pastor Noel moved out of their house which was much larger and into their mother's house that consisted of three bedrooms along with the guest wing. Rev. Jay's study consisted of the lounge area part of which Sherry converted into a studio, leaving the main half of it as a study. Their house had already been put onto the market by a reputable agent and one of their cars was already sold, fetching 0.7 million.

About eight months later, the other car was sold and there was an additional 1.2 million available for the building works, bringing the total fund raised to about 1.9 million. The project work continued for about one more month before it came to a standstill, yet again. Their house which was already on the market had not yet been bought. The offers made were so far too low and eventually when the house was bought at ten million Kenyan shillings, it was in the New Year and they had to divert the money towards the mission work that Woodlands City Congregation supported. They decided to be patient and take life as it comes.

Chapter 6

She was in a large desert, and nobody seemed to be in sight. She had been waiting for Eric who had gone a little ahead to look for some water. Suddenly, a gust of harsh desert wind started blowing, steadily becoming stronger. She heard the sound of hooves amidst the whirling wind and when it all quietened down she was aware of three hooded men, on horseback, looking down at her. The sun above was very hot and enervating. *It seems I am going to die before Eric returns with the water,* she thought and passed out. She awakened in her bed, drenched in sweat.

It had been a dream, she thought. Eric lay besides her, deeply asleep. She whispered a prayer of protection against the occurrences in the dream. Lately, Sheba's mind churned numerous fruitless thoughts. Her disposition was dull and her hands, normally busy, were lax.

Sheba had waited for this season to end like never before. Although she knew beyond the shadow of a doubt that life was worth a lot, the skies seemed dim above her head. *There is this verse in Deuteronomy that speaks about how my life is nowadays,* she thought. (Deut 28:66 NIV) *You will live in constant suspense, filled with dread both night and day, never sure of your life.* (Deut 28:67 NIV) *In the morning you will say, "If only it were evening!" and in the evening, "If only it were morning!" - because of the terror that will fill your hearts and the sights that your eyes will see. And yet these verses couldn't possibly be applying to me,* her thoughts went on, *I believe in God, I try to obey Him.* She longed for a child especially now, because she had everything she needed. She had laboured day and night to increase it and God had blessed her with wealth, health and good friends.

Her husband was loving and supportive. He did not pressure her at all. Adapting the life of a workaholic, continuous labouring had been her opium, her outlet.

"Sheba, please hurry," her husband's voice sounded from the living room, interrupting her thoughts.

It was then that she realised that she had been seated at her dressing table in front of the mirror for the last couple of minutes and her mind had wandered off again, her glazed eyes boring into and beyond the surface of the mirror.

She hadn't put on her makeup either. Startled into consciousness, she completed her beauty regimen with a heavy heart and emerged from the bedroom. They had been invited for a wedding and the day would be memorable. Weddings had a way of bringing together family and long term friends.

It was at this wedding that she saw Peter again. Peter was a gentleman with a light brown complexion and quiet mannerism; at least that was how he appeared to be.

Peter was quite likeable and he had prayed for her young cousin who was now getting married at her hospital bed when she had been ill. From time to time during their hospital visits, Eric and Sheba had encountered him.

"Hello Peter, *u hali gani*, how are you?" Sheba said.

"*Njema Mama*, I am alright Madam," Peter replied. '*Habari yako* Eric, how are you Eric?" Peter inquired.

"*Njema*, good," Eric replied.

'*Umepotea lakini!* You are so lost!" Sheba added.

"*Hujanialika kwako Mama.* You've not invited me to your house Madam," Peter replied.

"*Haya basi, nimekualika rasmi. Njoo ututembelee. Acha nikupe nambari yangu unipigie mara tu utakapokuwa tayari kuja.* Alright I now officially invite you. Come and visit us. Here is my number, call me when you are ready to visit and I will make time," she said as they exchanged numbers.

Her husband looked on curiously, never wanting to be an overly religious emotional zealot and yet aware of the cogent role that God and religion played in the scheme of things.

They smiled and moved on some steps passing greetings, hugs and kisses to friends and relatives before taking their seats.

*****

Eric had been talking to a friend at the close of the wedding reception when the sound of loud sharp laughter sounded from a group of three women. It was Sheba and her friends at a distance. The yellow and orange rays of the sunset hung in the horizon and the three women seemed quite happy. *Sheba is back to her bubbly and vivacious self, it seems*, he thought. And he was right. For some reason, after that particular wedding, Sheba became her old self again. She woke up early the next morning and, even though it had been a Sunday, she added some flower cuttings onto their flower bed before going to church.

And their nights were once again filled with bliss. She paid attention to detail again, even to Eric's wardrobe and diet.

*****

One rainy afternoon, Sheba's phone rang and it was Peter, the Pastor, or *Mtumishi Peter*, Servant Peter, as people liked to call him. He didn't mind the title either. He was ready to pay them a visit and possibly pray with them if they had any needs.

Peter had learned that in highlighting the possible empty places in another person's life, he kept them preoccupied and his own emptiness, namely poverty, would not be as glaring. This also kept some in their place, away from pride and they wouldn't begin to look down on him after receiving answers to what they had prayed for. He therefore usually stated the aim of his visit at the outset.

"*Umekaribishwa Peter, basi nitakungojea Alhamisi, lakini mbona usije jioni ili Mzee pia ajumuike nasi?* You're welcome Peter; I will wait for you on Thursday. However, wouldn't it be better if you came in the evening when my husband is back from work so that he can join us?" Sheba said.

"*Ingekuwa vyema lakini nina shughuli Alhamisi jioni nami sitaweza kukaa. Nina nafasi mchana.* Yes, that would've been great but I am busy on that particular Thursday evening and would therefore not be available, but I am free during the day."

"*Sawasawa nitakutarajia kwa chakula cha mchana, Ahsante.* Okay, I will be expecting you around lunch hour, thanks," Sheba confirmed their meeting.

"Asante, thank you," said Peter as he hung up.

Women are easier to minister to than men, he thought. *This is a matter of faith and it is better to speak to one with an open heart.*

*****

61

On Thursday, Sheba prepared herself fully having taken time to pray and fast on the previous day in order to have a more effective time of prayer with Mtumishi Peter. She helped her house help Mimo prepare a meal for lunch with Peter; chicken and salad with *Chapati*.[13] Peter arrived at about 12:30pm, in good time for lunch and they talked and shared from scripture. He emphasised that God was a God of results and that he had answered the prayers of every woman found in the Bible who was without a child and had prayed for one. He suggested that every Thursday they meet at Sheba's house for prayer and then wait and see what God would do for them. Sheba pondered for a minute or so.

She knew that her schedule gets quite busy sometimes but nevertheless, it would be worth the sacrifice to pray for her heart's earnest desire. She loved God so much.

"Okay, Peter, let me ask my husband if it is okay and I will let you know," she answered.

For a moment Peter's face darkened as a flicker of anger showed on his face and then it was gone as fast as it had come.

"It's okay Sheba, you go ahead and ask him and you will let me know," he answered.

It was about 4pm when they had read the Bible and prayed. "Mimo," Sheba called out for Mimo who had gone to the kitchen to wash the utensils that lay in the sink and to tidy the kitchen.

"Yes Mrs Sheba," Mimo answered.

"Please come," Sheba said.

"What do you prefer, tea or coffee?" Sheba asked Peter.

"I prefer coffee," Peter said.

---

13 A flat, fried Kenyan meal made of
    wheat and of Indian origin.

Mimo, a young girl of about 22 years of age presently came and stood before them, her dress wet near her waist and her eyes innocent. Sheba scolded her in her vernacular, regarding her omission of decorum as she didn't have her apron on, therefore making her dress wet. She ordered, "Mimo, please prepare a pot of coffee for Mtumishi Peter and some tea for us and warm some snacks as well."

"Yes Maam," she answered and immediately left to perform the task at hand. Feeling quite encouraged, and having some privacy as Mimo prepared the tea, Sheba began to pour out her heart some more to Peter as a grown up would speak to a counsellor.

Sheba's hand was adorned with beautiful gold wedding bands and her nails were well manicured. She wore a long embroidered tunic to her knees, and tights. The tunic was one of those classy African made ones, respectable on any woman.

Having an expensive weave on her hair, even without makeup, she was clearly a woman of means. She came across as wise too, having worked alongside her husband to reach their present status in life and not as those women who appeared pampered and yet foolish and without a clue as to what it takes to earn a decent living.

As she spoke, Peter marvelled at the needy state of human beings. No matter where one went, people seemed to have either one or more things lacking which if only they had, would complete their joy.

Mimo brought the hot coffee and tea with snacks and served them and then retreated to her quarters to continue with her other tasks. Sheba spoke and Peter answered with encouraging words of scripture. The issue of her childlessness and the pressure that came with that from the society came to the fore and as she unburdened herself once more, she felt somewhat lighter. Peter empathised deeply with her as the coffee pot emptied and time ticked away. As the conversation became lighter yet again, there was a knock on the door and Sheba looked at her watch. It was already 6pm and as she stood up to answer the doorbell she knew it would be Eric. Peter moved in his seat and shuffled his feet realising that he had overstayed as he had indicated he wouldn't be available in the evening.

Eric wore a big smile when he walked in and saw that Peter was in the house. "*Vipi Peter!* What's up Peter!" he said.

"I am fine *Mzee*," Peter answered, feeling relaxed at his welcome. "Was just leaving but since you are here and since it seems God wanted me to minister to your family today, I will stay on a little longer. I have had to cancel my earlier plans."

And so the evening wore on as they once again had dinner together.

Peter left at 8pm.

*****

"Peter wants us to lay more emphasis on prayer," Sheba suggested to Eric later as they went to sleep.

"Yes, I guess that's okay," Eric answered. "Incidentally, where does Peter go to church, is he a pastor?" he asked.

"Come to think of it, I don't know, I didn't ask, I have never asked," Sheba answered.

Eric dismissed the thought and shortly after, they were both asleep.

They were to continue with a series of meetings on Thursdays and Sheba had come to enjoy these times even though Eric was mostly unable to attend. Being generous, she would always make sure that Peter left with a package of goodies to eat and about a thousand shillings. She took it upon herself as a courteous act to one who was sacrificing his time and money to attend to her and join her in her faith as they prayed.

Peter had disclosed that sometimes he attended a church in the neighbouring estate but that he would soon be beginning a church as pastor.

*****

They had been through six months of this prayer routine and still there was no answer in sight when during one meeting, Peter felt that Sheba was getting desperate and he decided to make a proclamation by faith. It was during the December holidays and Sheba was getting ready to host her cousin's family for Christmas. Her children especially loved visiting Sheba. Mustering all his self-confidence, Peter spoke. "November next year Sheba, by November next year my sister, your prayer will be answered," he proclaimed to her.

He served God and he was sure that God would in turn fulfil a word that he had declared as his servant. He was confident about it.

Meanwhile, the Christmas holidays came and went and due to the nature of their business, Sheba found that she needed to travel quite a bit and when she came back, she would spend many hours supervising the immediate distribution of goods, monitoring the consignments to different parts of the country, conducting research on best prices and newer brands as business expanded. It was turning out to be quite a busy year and she was suddenly unavailable for any Thursday afternoon meetings at her home with Servant Peter. Sometimes, Peter would call her and try to get a conversation going but it proved futile to do so during the day and in the night she would either be dead asleep from exhaustion or she could only afford to have a mild conversation. Sometimes she would be in a remote place where the mobile service provider network was poor. Seven months had passed by in this state of affairs.

Her husband who was also her partner in business was likewise busy, supervising the building of a warehouse to help them increase their capacity and therefore avoid warehouse costs and the hurry to dispatch most of their goods at once. They had decided she would do the travelling in this season and he would supervise the building. The masons and other construction workers would respect Eric more and he would be more apt in monitoring quality and quantities of materials as well as the progress of the building while monitoring and reducing costs. The society was still very much patriarchal and though the woman had advanced, some areas were still tough to handle. They had agreed that it was best that Eric should handle a project of such magnitude.

It was late August when Sheba finally found herself back in her house with some time in her hands. It would take a while before the need for more goods to be distributed. They had made their shipping orders and usually, it took about three months for the delivery to be made for their type of goods after placing an order. She planned to engage a distribution and logistics manager in order to relieve her of this direct responsibility. The warehouse was undergoing final touches.

Mimo, her house help had tipped Servant Peter that Sheba was at home lately and he made his way to their home for fellowship.

*****

Sheba had begun to ponder servant Peter's words that she would be having a baby by November of that year. *I am definitely not pregnant and a child takes nine months in the womb after it is conceived. Evidently, I will not be having any child by November this year. Could it be that I heard wrongly?* she questioned. *But Eric heard it too.. Even though we haven't had any free leisurely time, we have had some time together. How is it that I am not pregnant and yet God promised ... how is it possible?*

*****

Servant Peter presently came, on a Thursday, and found Sheba at home. She was glad to see him, since it had been some time since they had met. It had actually been about eight months!

"Hujambo Madam Sheba, ni vyema sana kukuona, waendeleaje? Mbona katutupa hivyo? Hello Madam Sheba, it's so good to see you, how are you fairing on? Why have you been so quiet?" Servant Peter asked.

"I am fine Servant Peter. I have been very, very busy but I am well, God is good. How are you?" Sheba replied.

"I am okay as well," Servant Peter answered.

They had some refreshments and Mimo retreated to the kitchen to prepare dinner. They had some time of prayer, reading the Bible and singing. At about 5pm, as he indicated that he wanted to leave, Sheba decided to inquire about the utterance he had made the previous year.

67

"Well, Peter, I have been waiting on the Lord for what you had spoken to us about ... you know my issue?" she began hesitantly.

"Uh, wow! Is it already on course?" Servant Peter asked remembering what he had predicted.

Sheba drew a long breath and softly answered, "I am afraid not."

There was a moment of silence as Mtumishi Peter thought of what to say.

"You know for you to succeed, you have to take your time and relax and be in one place without the amount of activity and stress that you have undergone in the last several months. That may have been a hindrance you know ..." he trailed off.

Sheba pondered. "Okay, we will see what to do," she said, rising to bid him goodbye.

As they reached the door Servant Peter suddenly halted. *"Nimekauka sana, sijui kama waweza kunifadhili ka nauli?* I am really broke, Might you be able to help me with fare?" he asked.

"Oh!" she exclaimed. She had been deep in thought and it had escaped her mind that she should have given him some money.

"I'll be right back," she said and hastened to her bedroom. She came back with a one thousand shilling note and handed him another one hundred shilling note for easy change as is needed when using public transport.

As he left, she sat down in the living room to reflect. She resolved to take it easy for the next few months since she had concluded the heavy tasks by then and to nudge her husband to take some time off every so often. She perused her Bible and read the stories in the Bible concerning prophecies and how they came to pass. Many prophecies were recorded in the Bible, however, it was rare for a prediction to be made in the Bible and then to fail to come to pass. These thoughts disturbed her mind.

Leaving, Mtumishi Peter thought about Sheba's challenge. He was bewildered why his word had not come to pass and yet he was a servant of God. *The problem must lie with Sheba*, he thought.

*****

When next they met, Mtumishi Peter admonished Sheba, "Sheba, you need to have more faith in God and remember that to God, one day is like a thousand years and therefore God's timing is different from our timing."

"But Servant Peter, whenever there was a promise with a date in the Bible, the date predicted would not pass, you mentioned November in your word to me," she insisted. But sensing that her continued insistence would bring about acrimony, she changed the topic. "Let's have some lunch; I can smell that it is ready. Mimo!" she called.

"Yes Mrs Sheba," Mimo answered from the kitchen.

"Please bring the food to the table!"

"Yes Maam, it is ready."

They sat down to eat.

The silence at the table was almost becoming uncomfortable when Servant Peter spoke. "Maybe you should sow a seed as a sign of faith in God that you believe His word to you," he proposed.

"What do you mean? I tithe at my local congregation and I give offering too," Sheba answered.

"I know that you do but then look at your circumstances, your prayer hasn't been answered. It matters where you tithe. Anyway, I am not asking you to tithe to me if you don't want to," he continued. Sheba's forehead creased.

"Sowing a seed is simply giving a sizeable offering," he quickly explained, noticing her concern.

As they finished eating, Sheba pondered briefly and then went to her bedroom and took out her chequebook from her hand bag. She wrote Mtumishi Peter a cheque of ten thousand shillings, placed it in an envelope and went back to the living room. *After all, this gentleman is taking his time to stand with me in prayer,* she thought. *I might as well show my faith in God's word through him. However, I will tithe to Woodlands City Congregation. It is my local church.*

"Here you are Mtumishi Peter," she said. "This is the much I can sow for now."

Thirty minutes later, Servant Peter had excused himself in order to attend to a matter. He left the house and quickly rushed to the bank, reaching there five minutes to three o'clock, just before the doors were shut to clients.

*****

It was on a late February afternoon when suddenly Eric, who had been home, emerged from their bedroom fuming. He held a chequebook in his hand and her bank statement.

"Sheba do you mind letting me know what is happening between you and Peter?" he demanded in a low voice.

"Eric, surely you know that I do give some money to Servant Peter every now and then," Sheba answered.

"Yeah I know that honey but how did it get to a hundred thousand?" he said reading through the statement. "Ten thousand here, fifteen thousand, thirty thousand ..."

She sat still, dumbfounded.

"I don't want Peter coming to our home again," he said with finality. Sheba sat quiet, not wanting to argue. She knew when Eric had his mind set and would not budge. It suddenly dawned on her that she had actually spent a total of a hundred thousand Kenya shillings on Peter! *How is it that I forgot my statement and cheque book on the dressing table?* she thought.

When Mtumishi Peter next came to the house, Sheba disclosed to her that her husband didn't want any more meetings in their house and they would therefore have to stop. Servant Peter was angry about this sudden turn of events but he decided to take it calmly.

"Wow, is Eric looking for a blessing or a curse?" he said out aloud.

Sheba recoiled, "Peter, Godly people do not curse, they only bless." *How could he talk like that about my husband when all I have shared with him has come from Eric as well?* She wondered.

Servant Peter left. Sheba felt fed up and irritated. She made a decision to stop calling or meeting him for a while in order to clear her mind. After all, what he had spoken had not come to fruition.

"Maybe I can live like this," she said to herself. "If God wants to give me a child, He will and if not, let His will be done. I will not have anyone playing religious psychological games on me."

*****

After the incident, Servant Peter would call Sheba and she would give ambiguous one word answers. At times, she didn't pick up his call. She didn't send him any money as well. Slowly, the connection between them faded. She felt drained and cheated. Had she been taken for a ride? Her local church services, which hadn't been as interesting since she started meeting with Peter, suddenly felt more refreshing. She found that though Pastor Noel didn't bend to everyone's needs and whims, always offered guidance and had solid character. The church had a board of elders, deacons and staff. Pastor Noel was also their friend. He did not handle money directly but would only receive his salary. The account records were available for any church member to examine. He also worked with co-pastors, all trained in Bible school on various aspects of the Christian faith, including how to handle people. He seldom went to any congregant's house without a known cause and even more rarely would he go alone.

Ultimately it is important to put one's trust in God alone, Sheba thought as they sang the hymn *"On Christ the solid rock I stand, all other ground is sinking sand".*

*****

Mtumishi Peter sat in his one-roomed house. He was exhausted. Sometimes he had to walk for long distances to reach people for prayers. The rent, only three thousand shillings, was due and he didn't know where it would come from. He marvelled at how things were turning out.

72

I have stood by these Christians and yet they have mostly deserted me. They claim I am a false prophet and yet they themselves have not waited to see the words God had spoken come to pass, he thought, *such ungrateful and impatient people!*

To make matters worse, his former pastor has called him and invited him to go back to their congregation. *I can't go back to obey a man who is not as spiritually tuned to God as I am. I have a call to follow,* he thought. His former pastor had told Peter that by going out on his own without being accountable to anyone, he was in rebellion.

"You are an easy target for the enemy Peter," he had pleaded but Peter wasn't convinced. *Even when he had been in the church, his pastor had always been jealous that he, Peter, had more charisma and on occasion, he would speak a word and it would come to pass.*

Maria, his wife, had stepped out with some vegetables she had bought in the market in order to set up a stall in their estate and sell them. She had taken with her their two old son to her vegetable stall, a few yards from their house in order to sell and earn some profit. The profit mostly took care of their daily need for food, soap, cooking oil and other essentials but wasn't enough to cater for the rent and good clothing. For a while there she had thought that they were heading for better times as Mtumishi Peter seemed to have had quite a bit of money. It was from this money that he had given her three thousand shillings to start her green grocery business. Lately, however, he didn't return with any money in the evening. *Had God forsaken them?* She thought. *He couldn't!* She quickly discarded the thought.

Maria recalled a recent incident when she had to intervene in a situation. Mtumishi Peter had advised a neighbour who was encountering complications in her marriage to leave her husband. The woman had had a child before meeting him and the child was now sixteen years of age. However, the relationship with the child's father hadn't worked out well.

Mtumishi Peter had told her that she should go back to her first husband. However, the man had married and had two other children in his new marriage. It was twelve years since they had separated and the woman had been married to her present husband for exactly ten years with two children as well.

During their private talk as women, Maria prevailed on her neighbour to stay in her present marriage since every marriage encountered difficulties and furthermore, the man in question had remarried as well.

*****

One evening, Mtumishi Peter returned home with a tired but generous smile on his face. He was carrying shopping worth two thousand from a local supermarket. "Forget about those vegetables you're preparing," he told Maria. "I have bought some chicken and rice, that's what we will have for supper."

"Where did the money come from?" Maria asked.

"I met a man of God who understands what I am going through," he answered. "His name is Francis Katana and he is the apostle of a church called Assembly of Wonders and End Day Miracles."

"Isn't that the church that appears on a certain television channel on Saturdays? People are really talking about it, that they do a lot of exorcism and prophecy, and miracles happen there. I understand that they try to solve people's problems, individual by individual," Maria said.

"I don't know too much about the church yet," Mtumishi Peter said. "However, Apostle Francis himself understands the gift of prophecy very well and he has invited me to work with him. I will earn a salary..."

"Peter, I don't have a good feeling about this. How can a pastor offer you a job at his church when you scarcely know each other and without a recommendation from your former church? You may have some ability to give people prophecies but many times you have been wrong and you have not been accountable to any person other than yourself for a while," Maria stated.

At this Mtumishi Peter stood up, his eyes were red with anger and his tired demeanour made him look all the more dangerous and desperate. He looked at Maria menacingly, "Woman, do you know how far I walk and what humiliation I have to undergo day by day as I try to make ends meet. And now at last God has brought someone who understands me and wants to help me my way and you want me to let go of the chance to live a dignified life? Aren't you the one who's always asking me to go back to business in order to make ends meet instead of pursuing my calling? So why are you asking me to turn the opportunity of pursuing my calling and being paid for it pass by?" he shouted.

"It is okay Peter if you feel that this opportunity is God-sent," she said weakly. "Let me prepare the chicken!" she announced and retreated in fear to the space they had turned into a kitchenette.

Mtumishi Peter narrated to her how he had gone to the park that afternoon to preach to those who come there during their lunch break to take a rest. He had met Apostle Francis who had been passing by and had noticed him. Apostle Francis had waited until lunch hour was over and the people had dispersed in order to greet Mtumishi Peter. After introducing himself to Mtumishi Peter and asking him more about himself and his aspirations, he made him the offer to join him at his church.

On that Sunday, Maria had tugged along with her husband to church. Three months later, their lives had started showing as they became a little more comfortable.

*****

Sherry thought about the art exhibition as she lay on the bed. It was set to be held on the next weekend at Hotel Sebastian, a five star hotel partly owned by Samba More's family. Samba appreciated art and music and had bought some art pieces from Sherry in the past. Kipyegon, the Kenyan artist had completed his pieces and Jerome Nicholas and Martha Ferguson were set to come into the country on Wednesday of the following week. Charles Zuma, the South African, was already in the country. Their paintings had already been shipped prior to their arrival. It would have cost them much more if they had transported them by air due to their size. Maya Prikash from India and who was a South African of Dutch origin had also shipped in their art pieces.

The Hotel Sebastian had a magnificent ballroom where Sherry had opted to hold the exhibition. Samba had offered them the venue, cocktails, snacks and beverages for free. He did this as a gift to Noel Karo since he had not given him any upon his ordination. A lively band would be playing a range of pieces; from hymns to contemporary Kenyan, traditional hymns and American Christian music, especially the ones the late Rev. Jay Karo loved when he was alive. Another art exhibition would be held in New York at the university where Pastor Noel studied. Some pieces from Sherry Karo, Kipyegon and Maya Prikash had been shipped to the college to add on to some pieces that Martha Ferguson and Jerome Nicholas had painted.

When the day came, the air was festive and visitors began pouring into the venue. Some came to admire the art and give moral support and buy little art pieces while a few were seriously considering purchasing an art piece for a hefty amount. A word of prayer and worship music set the scene aright for the exhibition to begin. The guests were allowed to walk around and mingle while considering various art pieces and their corresponding prices. In two hours there would be a short speech by the chief guest and then the major sales incorporating an auction, would begin. The attendance was mainly by young people who had worked for a few years and wanted to have a peek at and identify with the finer things in life like art and middle aged people who had families and extra income. The other attendees were well established, wealthy individuals who loved art and were committed Christians.

The master of ceremony was a humorous middle aged man who had quite a wealth of knowledge in art. As the visitors stood to continue with the auctions, some were clutching their art pieces in their hands already. The auction began as the wealthy now bid for the centre pieces. The bidding continued for an hour and a half. Finally, the sales and accounts team deliberated on the amount that had been raised as the band played on. After half an hour, the music stopped. A total of two million Kenyan shillings had been raised in cash and five million in cheques. Another ten million had been pledged by those who had made down payments for the paintings in the form of cheques. The news was received with great applause and a thanksgiving speech by the organiser Sherry Karo and the visiting international artists ensued. Closing prayer followed and guests were allowed to leave at their leisure. Some decided to have dinner there as the day came to a close.

All in all, it had been quite a successful exhibition. If the money came in as it was expected, there would be a deficit of only about ten million shillings to raise and the work of building the church would soon be completed. The auction that had been held at college had brought in a total of ten million and those who purchased the art pieces had paid given cheques for the pieces bought immediately. However, the money in form of pledges would take a much longer time to come in and the additional ten million Kenya shillings would also take time to be realised. As another year passed, Sherry and Noel and all the leadership soon realised that God is not obliged to move things in the pace that we want him to. Process, it seems was of great interest to God just as the final outcome is. Woodlands City Congregation continued sending funds to the missions that they had been supporting, avoiding the temptation to withdraw support in order to complete their church auditorium earlier.

Chapter 7

✿

Eusebia dozed off as the sermon wore on. She sat at the back near the exit in order to make a quick take off if the baby began crying or disrupting the quiet atmosphere of the church. She loved God and religion. She loved the people in this church too, especially her boss' friends who would always say hello to her and speak a kind word. However, she understood close to nothing when it came to the sermon because she was illiterate, having been to school only up to class two and not having had the aptitude or the means to continue to learn by herself perhaps.

Eusebia was a typical country woman with cornrows and sometimes braids plaited on her naturally African hair. Luckily her hair was not the very kinky type but was soft and she could sometimes wash it at home. Her ebony complexion was flawless and she was of medium height and slightly plump, the perfect picture of health. Upon reaching puberty and entering into her teenage years, Eusebia found herself in an early marriage at the tender age of sixteen. Her father arranged for the marriage despite her mother's protests and as it was with many girls in her circumstances then, she had no further aspirations except to move to the next hierarchy of needs within her reach, which was marriage.

Ambrose, her husband, was twenty years old and had at least managed to complete his primary school education. He had worked for four years as a farm hand for a privileged family and had managed to buy two dairy cows. He sold milk to his neighbours. He seemed to be a man of vision and she counted herself somewhat lucky as she had not been married off to an old man. To top it all, her new husband had the most charming manner.

However, a few months into their marriage, Eusebia discovered that Ambrose had the peculiar behaviour of monitoring her use of household items including food which he would ration to her. By the third year of their marriage, Eusebia had given birth to two children, both daughters. Ambrose's veiled violent trait had come to the surface after her second child. Whenever they quarrelled, he would beat her and rape her.

She left her difficult marriage after five years, when her husband married another wife in order to look for a son. She took her children to her mother. Life was even more difficult and after about four years, at the age of twenty-six, her mother arranged for her to go to Nairobi and work for a distant relation who had married into another community.

She had worked for her distant cousin for a while until she got another job through a friend in a different neighbourhood. It turned out that George; her woman employer was a kind persona and treated her very well. George Mumbai was very light skinned and had short curly hair. Eusebia had wondered about her hair until George had told her that it was a curly kit and that her natural hair is very kinky. George was tall and slender and had keen eyes and a generous smile that lit her face. At George's house, Eusebia could eat as much as she wanted and cook food without rations being monitored. She had a good salary, rare among house helps then and could send about six thousand shillings home for the upkeep of her children. Her clothing was quite okay too. At first she had wondered why her boss's name was George, as she knew that George is a man's name but then she later learnt that her real name was Georgina and George was only a short form. Her husband would call her Georgina when in either extreme of his moods; when he was angry or very happy. On a daily basis, he would simply call her George. Georgina herself had to hold back from laughter when she first met Eusebia and learned her name. "Where did such a name come from?" George had wondered.

However, even though her financial situation was somewhat ameliorated, Eusebia had other problems that cropped up every now and then. She would get phone calls from her parents in the village regarding one issue or another which needed money. Some of her problems were especially difficult and she found it hard to share with her employer. Sometime back, her ex-husband had tried to forcefully take the two children from their grandmother's care and Eusebia had to travel home to solve the problem between her and Ambrose with the help of their families, the village elders and the area chief.

It was concluded that since Eusebia took good care of her children, they would remain in her custody through their grandmother and grandfather. During the sittings, it came to the fore that though he was still industrious, Ambrose was turning into a drunkard. He had had two more children with his second wife, one of whom was a boy. The village elders and the chief asked him to remain content with his new life.

George always said that the Bible had a solution to everything. Poor Eusebia, she couldn't read! *Had I the capacity to read or understand the Sunday sermon, then I would solve some of my problems*, she thought. However, George, though prosperous, had her own set of problems too.

81

Eusebia had heard a preacher quote a verse in Isaiah in Kiswahili, a verse which made a lot of sense to her. It was Isaiah 29:11-12. *"All these future events are a sealed book to them. When you give it to those who can read, they will say, 'We can't read it because it is sealed'. When you give it to those who cannot read, they will say, 'Sorry, we don't know how to read.'"*

The verse made sense to her. Therefore, even though George could read, the book must also be sealed to her since she isn't always apt at solving her issues either! Eusebia had watched George and her husband Michael arguing time and again. When it was really bad, they didn't eat together. She didn't always have a clue as to what they were arguing about since they mostly argued in English when they were really angry. They came from different ethnic communities and neither understood the language of the other. However, George's children had picked up quite a bit of her ethnic language. At least they could understand it and Eusebia spoke to them often. Since they would mostly answer her in English, she was beginning to pick up the basics of the English language in turn. Nevertheless, Eusebia had learnt to mind her own business when it came to George and Michael, sometimes they would be the best of friends in the morning after having a bitter argument the previous night, holding hands like little children. Sometimes Michael had the audacity to kiss George in her presence, as if she was invisible. He did this especially when they had agreed after quarrelling or when he was about to travel for a week or so. Eusebia hated it when he did that and she would exit the living room. *"Nyenya Michael ambe i time yanje, nyanzile sikila ali ne milimo milai* but the family needs him too, we need to spend time together," George once mentioned to Eusebia in vernacular and English. "I appreciate that Michael has a wonderful career but I want him to spend more time with us."

All in all, Eusebia felt that George had a life with less stresses. She would always find a way of accomplishing what she wanted, whether it was buying a consignment of goods and selling them to her contemporaries or planting a crop in their farm up country. George was a nurse at a private hospital but she also had some free time whenever she was off duty. She always had a book or two which she read when the children were away to keep her busy. She did a lot of work for her local church including baking goodies to give away, donating clothing items, teaching a class and so on. George's friends were mostly like her, in that; they kept talking about their children, interesting things to do and places to go.

Eusebia had found herself almost being ostracised when she had first come to the city. The relative she had worked for lived in an average estate. The little houses which were in close proximity had two bedrooms each and the larger ones had three bedrooms. The compounds were tiny. She would prepare the children for school, a four year old boy who went to kindergarten and a nine year old girl in primary school, do the housework and go to sleep. She didn't know anyone but gradually she got to know fellow house helps and they would greet each other and exchange small talk.

Trouble had begun when her relative lost her job when the company she was working for shut down. She had more time at home and therefore more time to interact with her neighbours, some of whom were housewives.

In the afternoons, a visitor would come and say hello. Later two women visitors would come and then three. It became habitual and the more they interacted, the more they discussed irrelevant topics. The topics ranged from how unfashionable one of their neighbours was to how desperate another whose husband had been cheating on was.

Eusebia usually preferred to be asleep until the children came back from school. She had come to loathe the topics. *It is pointless to talk about something that is of no benefit whatsoever,* she thought. *A person should speak about something only once but if the talk continues and the person has no power to change or help the situation at hand and to make the matters worse, if the situation is not any of a person's immediate business; it is pointless, demeaning and sometimes hateful to the subject. I am always left with a bad taste in my mouth in such discussions.*

As she interacted with fellow house helps, it was expected of her to engage in all manner of gossip and when she didn't, she noticed, they would avoid her. However, in George's neighbourhood, the houses were a bit far apart and it was more difficult to interact purely for small talk. *If such women who love to gossip are here in this neighbourhood, then they are not George's friends,* she thought.

Sudden news had sent Eusebia into turmoil and confusion. She was told that her eldest daughter, 15 year old Rose, was not feeling well and she urgently had to go to the village and see her.

A long journey, about seven hours to her home in the western part of the country ensued and on reaching home, she found her mother and father in a sombre mood.

"Hello mother, I am here now," she greeted her mother. "What has happened with Rose? Where is she ill?"

"Sit down my child," her mother replied. "Rose is very ill, she seems to have lost her mind!"

"Lost her mind because of what? That's impossible!" having observed George, she had learnt not to panic in critical situations. "*E problem yosi ebeye ne solution mama.* Every problem has a solution mother," she found herself echoing George's words. "Have you taken her to hospital?" she inquired.

"No!" her mother answered.

"We're taking her to hospital mother," Eusebia stated.

She had come with fifteen thousand shillings. She hoped it would be enough for treatment and food for her daughter and her transport back.

Eusebia was overcome with shock when she saw her daughter. She quickly pulled herself together and they rushed her to the mission hospital nearby where treatment began. Besides the fever, nausea and dizziness, Rose was exhibiting weird symptoms like speech impairment, epilepsy and hyperactive, irrational behaviour. The doctor attended to her and gave her some drugs which seemed to help her for a while and she was discharged. However, one week later, the symptoms recurred.

Eusebia had spent eight thousand Kenya shillings in this entire ordeal and now she didn't know what to do. She stayed on for another week to observe how her daughter would progress. They had to restrain her from removing all her clothes sometimes as she broke down and cried. On other times, she drooled or she would burst into sudden intense laughter. She remained unable to speak.

Eusebia and her mother resorted to prayer and waited to see if there would be a change in Rose. However, there seemed to be none. A neighbour had suggested they join the African Church Sect, which was a cocktail of ancestor worship, African traditional religion and many aspects of Christianity and Judaism. They however believed themselves to be a church. She told them that a prophet would attend to them and pray for her daughter.

Although they belonged to a church with an Anglican background, being desperate, they accepted the invitation. They were required to wear white gowns and headscarves similar to those of nuns, with a red stripe on the headscarf and a red belt around the waist. They obliged and attended the service.

*****

Here, it was a matter of singing spiritual songs in mother tongue until one was fever pitch. Eusebia watched as some men and women worked themselves up into a frenzy. The more one worked themselves into frenzy, the more they were deemed to be in the spirit and appeared to be admirable to the rest. When everything quieted down, all attention was on the leaders and prophets of the sect who could solve a myriad of problems and even foretell the future through prayer, it was claimed.

Eusebia and her mother's turn came and they presented their problem. Rose who was slightly calm on that day was prayed for and the prophet stated that Rose would recover and gain her sanity. One thing that Eusebia liked about this sect was that they read from the Bible in Swahili and mother tongue, and even preached in mother tongue which she could understand. She didn't like the clothes though.

Surprisingly, during the following week, Rose did not improve but seemed to get worse.

*****

It had been almost a month since Eusebia had taken leave to go and attend to her daughter. On that Friday, when George called her as she usually did to find out how things were fairing, Eusebia disclosed to her that it seems Rose, her daughter, had gone mad and she didn't know what she should do.

"Mad? What would make her go mad?" George asked. "Is it possible to bring her here to Nairobi to check her thoroughly before making that final conclusion?" she asked her.

"I don't know Madam George," Eusebia answered. "I will see if it is possible."

On that Saturday, similar to the emergence of a clear sky after a storm, Rose suddenly calmed down.

"George, my Madam, has asked me to try and get Rose to Nairobi and she will take her to the doctor where they will conduct a thorough check-up on her. I am taking Rose on today's night bus. George will take us to the doctor first thing in the morning tomorrow, since it's a Sunday and she won't be at work," Eusebia told her mother.

"It's alright my dear. Since Rose is always seemingly getting better and then worse, it would do her some good to be checked by better doctors in the city," her mother replied.

The pair hastened to get Rose ready and make the trip to the bus station to secure a place in the evening bus. As usual George, as keen as ever, was waiting for them and had alerted her doctor in the private hospital about Rose, Eusebia's daughter. On arrival, she picked them up from the bus station and they headed straight to the hospital.

*****

Rose, who had begun to show symptoms of hyper active behaviour, was calmed and admitted and after interrogating Eusebia thoroughly on Rose's condition, the doctor dismissed the two and they left the hospital.

George looked at Eusebia in empathy, marvelling at how ill-equipped she seemed to be to handle her present situation and how exhausted she was. When they got home, she served her a meal and Eusebia retreated to her quarters, took a shower and slept soundly.

She woke up early the next day and began her household chores. George had indicated that she would be back from work by around 12pm when they would go to the hospital and check on her daughter. When she came back at 12:15pm, George seemed more relaxed than she had been the previous day and she told her that they would go to the hospital together. The doctor had told her that they had finally found out what Rose was ailing from.

Upon reaching the hospital, the doctor explained to George and Eusebia in turn that Rose had cerebral malaria and that they had begun treating her. It would take therapy even after treatment for her to fully regain her faculties.

On their way home, Eusebia inquired, "So this cerebral malaria has symptoms similar to madness?"

"Yes my dear," George answered, "but don't worry, she will be fine in due time. We will pray for her, even with my church fellowship."

Two weeks later, Rose was discharged and brought to her mother's one bed-roomed servant's quarters. There she recovered gradually with the help of a therapist who came once a week for the next six weeks. She stayed on for another month until she was bright and healthy again. She had missed a full school term and that meant she would have to study that particular term's work during the entire school holiday in order to try and catch up with her peers.

Her teachers in the village were sympathetic towards her situation since she had been a promising student. They therefore agreed to assist her even after the schools opened for the third term of school until she caught up with the rest of the students. The treatment had cost a lot of money but since Georgina was a nurse at the hospital, it had helped. Eusebia could not pay her back for her daughter's treatment but she vowed within herself to work for George better than ever. A stronger bond of loyalty that would be tested in due time had resulted between the two women.

One Sunday, after the incident and Eusebia was back to her usual self, George was surprised to see her dressed in a flowing white dress and matching headscarf with a red stripe and a red belt.

"Eusebia, what could be the matter? Aren't you coming with us to church?" George asked. George's daughter Blanche and her son Nandi, who were both in their teens, laughed hard at Eusebia's attire. Having returned from boarding school, they found this latest development in Eusebia quite entertaining.

"Madam Georgina, this is the church I went to at home in the village when Rose was sick and the prophet predicted to me that she would be healed and she was healed. I have been told that I have to attend here since they have several congregations even in the city."

"I know God healed your child but even then you didn't need a prophet to tell you that she would be healed. In any case it was the doctor's treatment and the therapy that brought about the healing. Don't you think God might have used the doctor as opposed to the prophet? Don't you know this group is a cult?" George answered her, irritated.

"Madam, they read the Bible in Swahili and Luhya. They also pray just like other people, they are not a cult group," she answered.

"So where are you going, so that I can drop you off? Where is the nearest congregation?"

"Madam George, you just drop me off at the bus stop and I will get means to the congregation. It is at Sabuni slums," she answered. Her answer sent George's kids into another round of laughter.

"Eusebia, Eusebia!" George muttered. "Okay everybody, let's go," she ordered and they all got into the car. George's husband was out of the country on official duty. Eusebia picked up Cherie, the little four year old and they got into the back seat with Blanche as Nandi sitting at the front. She dropped Eusebia off at the nearest bus stop.

Eusebia had almost forgotten about that group until she received a call from the Prophet Marko Yohana, who reminded her that he had prayed and predicted her daughter's well-being. "Don't turn your back on the true God and his servants," he had said.

"Prophet, indeed my daughter is well, but there is no such congregation here," Eusebia had replied, glad to escape the entrapment.

"Eusebia, you can always send your tithe by the instant money transfer service available on your phone network and let me surprise you, there is a congregation of our faith near you, at Sabuni slums!"

"Do I have to go there?" Eusebia inquired. "I already go to the church where my madam goes…"

"Eusebia, fear the Lord… fear the Lord! I am sure you want to honour your child's healing…" Prophet Marko Yohana had said.

Eusebia was filled with fear. According to her observation, Yohana Marko was revered by the sect members back at the sect in the village. *It is no wonder he is known even here in Nairobi,* she thought.

True to her thoughts, she received a phone call from the sect leader at Sabuni slums who informed her that Marko Yohana had spoken to him about her and that they were expecting to see her at their service on that Sunday.

George pondered about Eusebia as she drove to church. She had heard of audio bibles. *These are indeed useful for all of us, especially for those who are illiterate and cannot read or those who are blind,* she thought. She purposed to get a copy for Eusebia. *Eusebia is quite intelligent and I know she can at least understand the Bible if she listened to it, I don't want a blind sect follower in my house. Who knows where it will all end,* she wondered.

In the bus, Eusebia sat next to a lady. She was dressed in similar fashion.

"*Habari yako,* hello?" she started. The lady answered the greeting and they began to chat. Her name was Serah. She was from a different community. As Eusebia looked closer, she noticed that though their garb was similar, there was a mild

91

difference in their patterns. Both their dresses were long and flowing and they both wore white headscarves. Eusebia's dress had a red band and her neighbour's was pure white.

*****

She entered the church and was greeted and asked to introduce herself and when the sect leader heard her name he understood that she was the one who had been sent by Yohana Marko, John Mark.

Eusebia was glad to meet with members who seemed to all come from her community. Songs were sung to the rhythm of a traditional drum as members sang themselves hoarse and danced energetically. They met under a tree besides an iron sheet structure that was being built. After the singing, there was a session of prayer and exorcisms which seemed to be quite dramatic and confusing. The members then began confessing their sins publicly. Some spoke of covetousness and asked for forgiveness. Some spoke of lust and some of desiring worldly success and they too asked for forgiveness.

By then Eusebia was losing concentration and though she enjoyed listening to the word in her language, it came up at the end of the service when she was exhausted and dozing. She couldn't make head or tail of what was being said either. Nobody seemed to be reading and referring to their bibles as she had become accustomed to in George's church. The pastor seemed to be speaking of a man having many wives.

It was 3:00 pm when the service came to an end after what seemed to be an eternity. Eusebia was about to leave when Meshech, the pastor, beckoned to her and when she went there, he invited her to stay with the leaders and their wives as they had lunch.

Eusebia sat down to eat and they had *ugali,* vegetables and chicken.

They also drunk sodas, and as it got late, she asked to leave.

"My boss will be expecting me by 6:00pm," she said.

"You live at their house?" Meshech asked.

"Yes," she answered.

Reluctantly, they allowed her to leave. Eusebia left at 5:00pm and took a bus back to the estate. She entered her little house and removed her shoes, immediately she jumped on the bed, exhausted. It was one hour later when she awoke to the sound of her mobile phone ringing. It was George.

"Eusebia, are you back? Did you manage to buy some tomatoes?"

"Oh!" she sighed. Amidst all the activities, she had forgotten to get tomatoes as George had requested her to from the market located near where her new church was.

The next week Eusebia carried out her chores with grace as usual and made sure that everything was up to standard just like Madam George liked it. She had been a little overwhelmed when her child had been sick and George had understood and hired extra help from a lady who would come in the morning to help with the housework and then leave afterwards. However, now that she felt better, she thought it would be prudent to work hard in gratitude. She knew that George could fuss sometimes, especially when the work was not being done to her satisfaction.

On the next Sunday, Eusebia wore the white regalia and headscarf and prepared to leave for church. Michael and George had travelled since Friday afternoon and would be coming back on Sunday evening. She got out of the house, locking everything up and saying hello to Alfayo, the day guard, she walked to the bus stop.

*****

Meshech was delighted to see her. Though just a house help, Eusebia enjoyed a little more comfort than those who lived in Sabuni slums and its environs. During the previous week, Meshech had showed up at her employer's house while George was away. It was 11am and Eusebia had just completed her tasks and was relaxing while having a cup of tea with the gardener and security guard outside in the garden. There had been a knock at the gate and the security guard had gone to check who it was that had knocked instead of ringing the bell. He had opened the gate and there Meshech stood.

"I am looking for Eusebia, I understand she works here," he inquired.

"Yes she works here, but who are you? Who should I say is looking for her?"

"Tell her it's Meshech," he had answered with a smile and great confidence.

Eusebia had panicked upon hearing that a man named Meshech was looking for her and that he seemed to belong to a certain sect. She had quickly took off her apron and wiped her mouth with the back of her hand. *What could Meshech want and who showed him where I work?* Eusebia had wondered. She had hastened to the gate and there Meshech was. He had looked at her and stretched his hand in greeting.

Suddenly she was conscious of her mode of dress. She had put on a flowery knee length cotton frock and sandals which showed the purple nail polish which she had applied. George had bought it for her. She didn't have her headscarf on either

94

and her neat cornrows with dark maroon braid additions were exposed. Although the sect was against this form of embellishment, Meshech didn't seem to mind. Eusebia's mind was going helter skelter as she tried to figure out what to do since she knew that her employer could drive into the compound at any time as was characteristic of her. George Mumbai did not approve of the sect and would not be happy to find Meshech and Eusebia standing outside her gate chatting.

"Meshech it's good to see you, how did you find out where I am working?" she asked, closing the gate behind her.

"There is a member who works close to this place and she told me she had seen you in this neighbourhood. However, she lives at Sabuni slums and commutes daily," he answered. "Is there anything wrong with my coming to visit you? Don't you receive visitors?"

"Actually, I don't receive visitors as such and besides my Madam does not approve of your church," she answered. "I don't want to lose my job or get into trouble," she quickly added.

"We can walk as I take you to the bus stop, we will meet on Sunday" she said.

Meshech frowned and walked alongside Eusebia. His face reflected disappointment and reluctance but he had no choice but to oblige as he noted Eusebia's worried expression that continued to build up. In his mind, he had planned to spend this day with Eusebia. He was hoping to enjoy some tasty food and a chat with her before her employers came back.

"You see Meshech, my employer comes in any time of day to check on things so it isn't good for people to visit me at work," she clarified.

They approached the bus stop and Eusebia took out her purse from the pocket of her cotton frock and fished out a fifty shilling note. "Let's go to that shop in the distance so that I can at least buy you a soda," she said.

Meshech was already hungry and thirsty and so he followed her to the shop where she bought him a bottle of fanta and cake and he sat down at the bench beside her to drink it. Eusebia fidgeted hoping that George would not drive by at that moment but in case she did, she had decided that she would tell her that Meshech was a distant relative. After about ten minutes, he had finished taking the drink and they proceeded to the bus stop. A bus heading to Sabuni slums approached and Eusebia fished out another fifty shilling note and handed it to Meshech for his bus fare back. He shook her hand.

"See you on Sunday," she blurted and let out a deep sigh as she hurried back to the house.

Sunday did come and as she said hello to the women and sat on the side where women sat, Meshech had his eyes intently fixed in their direction but she acted as if she didn't notice. The chatter quieted down as the service began. The drumming and dancing went to hysterical levels as they sang praises. Afterwards, there was a myriad of prophecies ranging from what would happen in the country to individual ones which included who had been bewitched and mention of those who had cast a spell and then there were prayers to set the bewitched persons free from the spells.

The sermon began and Eusebia steadied herself to sit up and pay attention. She was tired but not as much as she had been the first time she attended the service. Meshech began to preach citing a passage of scripture which Eusebia scarcely knew. As the message carried on Eusebia began to get the gist of Meshech's sermon. He urged the listeners to choose whom they will serve just as Joshua in the Bible did; whether they would serve God or men.

"A person may pretend to serve God on Sunday but during the week their behaviour is worldly and their dressing like that of a loose woman. Some value their worldly positions, jobs and wealth more than they value their God. It is time to choose," he thundered. "It is time to choose what is more valuable to you; whether God or men, positions, jobs and wealth. Choose God and throw the other things away."

Eusebia's heart sunk as she lowered herself in her seat. *Was the tirade directed at her or was it sheer coincidence?* Her mind was beginning to get preoccupied on thoughts on whether she would endure as a member of this particular church. She felt like it would be a heavy burden to bear.

Eventually, the sermon came to an end. It was 3pm, and as they stood to sing, Eusebia resorted to leave immediately after the benediction. She didn't have that sweet elated feeling that she felt whenever a service came to an end, especially when they had gone to Madam George's church. However, as she shook her neighbour's hand, before she turned to leave, a woman called her aside and informed her that she would be having lunch with Meshech and the other leaders once again. This would be the third Sunday in a row where she had ended up having lunch with Meshech and the other servants of God. The stout woman held her hand and gently led her in the direction of the tent where they would have their lunch. This time they had prepared a spiced meat and rice, which was a coastal dish known as *pilau*. She sat nervously and graciously accepted the rice heaped on her plate even then knowing that she wouldn't be able to finish the food but feeling too intimidated to ask the server to reduce the portion on her plate.

They ate for a long time and just as she thought it was time to leave, it was announced that there was tea to follow. At 4:30pm the tea was served. Eusebia gulped down the tea and followed one of the women who had served her, and who happened to be Meshech's wife as well, out of the tent to assist a little in washing the dishes. She did so and afterwards asked a young girl to get her bag from inside the tent. After a few minutes, the girl brought the bag and Eusebia sneaked through a narrow path to the bus stop where she got into the first bus that was headed to George's house. However, she remembered that she needed to buy a few green groceries and she got off at the nearby market to replenish the onions, tomatoes and other vegetables. She boarded another bus and got home by 6:30pm with all that George had requested her to get from the market. After dropping the groceries at George's kitchen, she went out to have a chat with the security guard and prepared a late cup of tea for both of them. She wasn't planning to prepare supper since she had had a late lunch and was tired from the day's activities as well. At 7:30pm, Michael and George drove into the compound. They had gone on safari to the Mara game reserve with Cherie since the other children were back in school.

Eusebia dutifully welcomed them, taking their bags and bringing them to the kitchen, which she had opened. They got into the house and as Michael and Cherie went on into the house to relax and get changed, George took out a small pizza and handed it to Eusebia, instructing her to share it with the guard. "I am really tired and so are you. We'll talk tomorrow," George told her.

"Okay Madam, and thank you," Eusebia answered and went outside to give the night guard some pizza to have with the tea they had made. She would eat hers for breakfast on the next day.

On Monday morning, Eusebia got up and performed her tasks as usual. George soon came down to have breakfast with Michael and Cherie before dropping off Cherie to school. Today she was off duty and she would therefore have time to rest and perform useful tasks around the house. Eusebia liked it when George took time to spend the day in the house since she had someone to converse with and have lunch with during the day. She cleaned the breakfast utensils and sat down at the dining table to have some tea and pizza from the previous day. George walked in and went upstairs. She came down with a package and gave it to Eusebia. It contained a t-shirt that they had bought from the Mara and a cd. George went to the cd player and promptly placed the cd which started playing. It was an audio Bible in Kiswahili. The voice that read the Bible was warm and inviting.

"Eusebia, I want you to be listening to this Bible readings since it they will help you understand the word even though you cannot read much," George said.

Eusebia who had been admiring the t-shirt sat up and her face lit up in a smile. "Madam George, you mean there is such a thing...that a person can actually listen to the Bible instead of reading it?" she exclaimed.

"Yes indeed Eusebia, at least for a start. Maybe you could learn to read and write a little later. Would you like that?" she asked.

"Yes, but I will not learn with kids and I will not wear any uniform," she said.

"Okay then, you will when the time comes," George assured her.

"Madam, I had such a terrible time yesterday at pastor Meshech's church," Eusebia started.

"Really, what happened?" George asked.

Eusebia narrated to her how Meshech had visited her during the week, how the Sunday service had been and the content of Meshech's sermon.

"Wow, Meshech seems quite manipulative to me," George stated. However, she did not continue with the conversation. Eventually, Eusebia would have to choose where she wanted to worship. George stepped out to go and carry out some errands leaving Eusebia listening to the audio CD for about an hour as she did her tasks. Eusebia quietly considered George's life. Despite her shortcomings and problems, she was a godly woman no doubt. Her dressing wasn't that much traditional but it was decent and creative too. Presently, George had coloured her hair with henna and Eusebia thought it looked quite good. Inevitably, by virtue of her clothing, Meshech would not consider George a woman of faith.

*****

The week had been especially pleasant as it was when Michael had not travelled. *There is something quite exciting and different when Michael and George are both around,* Eusebia thought. *I think the father of a house also carries a presence and an anointing,* she concluded.

Sunday had come once again and they all got ready to leave for church. Michael almost choked on his coffee as Eusebia walked past him into the kitchen in her flowing robes and headscarf. He laughed out for a long time until George came down to find out what was so hilarious. It was the first time he was home on a Sunday since Eusebia started attending the sect.

"Eusebia!" he called out.

"Yes, Sir Mumbai," she answered and came to the living room.

"Why are you dressed like that?" Michael asked her.

"The church that I go to nowadays requires that we dress in these clothes," she answered. "Didn't Madam George inform you that I moved to another church?"

"I didn't remember to tell Michael," George answered. "Anyway you finish whatever you were doing since we are leaving in ten minutes. I will drop you at the bus stop," she said. Eusebia retreated to the kitchen and George lightly reproved Michael for his reaction. Nevertheless Eusebia had not taken offense since he knew that Michael Mumbai was quite a humorous person.

They left for church. George felt quite blessed and relieved to have Michael driving for a change. They dropped Eusebia at the bus stop and continued on to Woodlands City Congregation. Eusebia got to church and said hello to the few acquaintances she had come to know, most of whom were women. Pastor Meshech was there as usual as well as the other pastors and leaders. The service went underway and Eusebia did her best to sweat it out with the rest of the congregation, during praise and worship. When the time for prophecy

101

came, a few men and women went into a trance and began to prophesise.

"Meshech receive your reward as a faithful man; receive the widow Eusebia into your care as your wife Meshech just as Boaz received Ruth. The Lord has spoken!" one of the pastors announced.

A sharp pain went through Eusebia's heart and she felt as if she would faint. The congregation clapped their hands and said Amen.

Other prophecies concerning other individuals and other matters went on but Eusebia hardly paid attention. She felt like a deer which a lion was just about to pounce on. She contemplated walking out but decided that it would be too dramatic and it may bring a curse upon her from God's servant. After all it was he who had prayed and Rose had been healed. *The medicines had worked on her Rose too*, she thought and dismissed that thought altogether. She was sweating profusely as the prophecies ended and they sang a song and sat down to listen to the sermon.

Another pastor gave the sermon this time and just as it was coming to a close, Eusebia had made a decision. She would pretend to go to the latrine and escape. She would not have lunch with the pastors and their families today. She sneaked out when everybody had bowed down their heads in prayer to conclude the service. She walked calmly in the direction of the pit latrines as if she was going to relieve herself but just as she got there she got into the alternative pathway nearby and broke into a run. On reaching the bus stop, she boarded a vehicle to town. Once she got to town, she had decided that she would pay her cousin an impromptu visit and ask for her advice on what had just transpired.

Her cousin was surprised to see her but nevertheless, she welcomed her and they had lunch together. She lived in a small but neat house and had two children and a good husband. Her cousin had also been lucky enough to complete her education and was a primary school teacher. After they had spoken about their families and general matters, Eusebia told her the story of Rose's illness, her connection with the African Church sect, the recent occurrences and that day's prophecy. Her cousin listened to the story with patience and fascination but later dismissed the prophecy and told Eusebia to beware of people who controlled others using religion. Eusebia felt relieved, courageous even to disobey the prophecy. They had tea at 5pm and she left to return to her house.

She arrived at 6:30pm and retreated to her quarters to rest until the next day. Monday morning, George was off duty again. They enjoyed the day as George went to do her errands and came back in the afternoon.

On Tuesday late morning as Eusebia sat to have tea with the gardener and Alfayo, the day guard, there was a knock on the gate. Alfayo walked to the gate to check who was knocking and there stood Meshech.

"*Dada Eusebia yuko*? Is sister Eusebia in?" he asked.

Alfayo looked at him nonchalantly, "Yes, wait here, I will let her know you have come," he replied. He locked the gate and went to the garden.

"That man is back again, the one called Meshech and he is asking for you," he said to her.

"What!" Eusebia almost choked on her tea. She took off her apron, went into the house and changed into a long dress. She rummaged her drawer for her headscarf but did not find

103

it. She stopped looking upon recalling that she had just washed it with the laundry. Walking fast to the gate, she stepped out. Meshech was sitting on the cement at the side of the gate where there was some shade. On seeing her, he stood up and straightened his flowing garments, a light pink cotton robe with a red cross at the right side of the chest. He wore a trouser inside and flowing head garb with a cross at the front. He wore strong boots which signified he had not changed shoes upon leaving work as he worked as a night guard.

"Eusebia, how are you?" he asked.

"I am fine pastor Meshech. My madam shouldn't find us here," she quickly added.

She began walking towards the bus stop and Meshech followed.

"What happened on Sunday?" Meshech asked.

She froze on the pathway and mustering courage, she turned to face Meshech. "I had to leave early and come back to work."

"So what did you think about God's will for us?" Meshech persisted. "You know I love you, don't you," he said trying to reach out for her hand.

Eusebia felt confident enough to mouth the words she had rehearsed for the past 36 hours.

"I don't love you and I won't marry you," she said quietly.

"Eusebia, do you want to disobey God even after the miracle you saw in your life when Rose was healed. Since then I know that your income has also increased, all God's blessings due to the prayers of his servant Yohana Marko and I," he concluded.

"It is well Pastor Meshech, you have a wife and in the New Testament, the Bible commands that one who serves in the church should be the husband to one wife," she said.

"When did you ever read the Bible? Do not allow yourself to be deceived by anyone…" Meshech stated contemptuously. "Remember that Ananias and Sapphira died by disobedience to the Lord just as Lot's wife did," he stated.

A strong mixture of fear and defiance rose within Eusebia. "I don't care about those people you are saying and I will not marry you or come to your church henceforth!" she said and quickly marched away back to the house. Meshech tried to grab her arm but she swung it loose and continued walking.

"Eusebia…" he shouted and stood for a minute. He contemplated following her back to the house and decided otherwise.

Her heart was beating rapidly and though she was afraid, she resolved to face the consequences of her action later. *Maybe God will listen to me because though I was happy to have my daughter healed, I do not want to belong to this sect at all,* she thought. At the back of her mind, she had noted the names Ananias and Sapphira as well as Lot. She would find out what these people did in the Bible. She remembered Pastor Noel Karo from George's church saying that God will never force somebody to do something against their own volition.

Eusebia arrived at the gate looking ruffled, to the amusement of Alfayo the guard.

"Why is your forehead creased like that? You look so worried," Alfayo asked her.

"Never mind," Eusebia answered and went to the garden. She sat where she had been. Her tea had gone cold and she no longer had the desire for it. Alfayo and the gardener had already finished having theirs. She poured it on the grass, went to the kitchen, poured herself some juice and returned to take it quietly. *I will make sure I listen to the words of the Bible at least for one or two hours daily; in the morning when I am cleaning up in the kitchen and in the late afternoon when I am resting, before Cherie comes home,* she thought. She also resolved to visit Woodlands City Congregation church office and book an appointment to see the pastor for advice and counselling as she had often seen George do in her times of need.

*****

Pastor Noel gave a warm smile to Eusebia when she came into his office on a Thursday afternoon. She asked Mary to organise a cup of coffee and snacks for Eusebia. He held Eusebia in high esteem for her devotion towards the family that had employed her, the Mumbais, and her willingness to help others in the community as well at their times of need.

Eusebia narrated to Pastor Noel what had happened after her child was healed of cerebral malaria and how she had found herself attending the African Traditional Church of Jesus Christ. She inquired from him the differences between what was genuine Christian and what was not. He explained to her that the sect she had began attending was a mixture of African culture and Old Testament cultural practices. The cult embraced the concept of salvation through Jesus Christ. He further explained to her that it was not true that she would die as Ananias and Sapphira had died as written in Acts chapter 5 in the Bible.

Sell Me a Prayer

Pastor Noel charged Eusebia with the task of gathering her colleagues who came to church at Woodlands City Congregation and were challenged in understanding the English services whether fully or in part. He invited them for lunch to his house on the next Sunday after the services were over. He desired that they should form a cell group to enable them share and listen to scripture passages together, to discuss and ask any of the pastors for further elaboration where it was needed. Eusebia left the pastor's office after prayer. She had expected that Pastor Noel would scold her for attending services elsewhere but instead, she he had reassured her.

Eusebia went on to invite, Tom, Sherry Karo's cook, who would be charged with the task of preparing lunch for the group. She also invited Mimo, Alfayo, the day guard, and Salome, an older house help like herself. When they gathered at Pastor Noel's house, it was decided that they should meet once a week just as the other groups met and they should hold activities together as well.

Alfayo, who had completed his secondary school education and could read and understand both English and Kiswahili languages, was made leader of the group. He would be assisted by Eusebia. To Pastor Noel's surprise, Alfayo's face lit up at the decision to make him the leader of the group. Hitherto, Alfayo had thought his education almost wasted but this new role infused him with fresh vigour and a new outlook. Three weeks later on a Saturday afternoon, the group held their first Bible study meeting. There were Bibles in Swahili and vernacular for those who understood the languages and audio Bibles in Swahili as well available for distribution.

As Alfayo and Eusebia had worked closely in the past three weeks to bring the programme together, it had become clear to

107

Pastor Noel that they had unique spiritual gifts. Eusebia had a growing gift of prophecy and once grounded in the word she would be able to use it better. Indeed, she had admitted to have found this gift of help to her and others especially through dreams and what she had classified as instinct over the years but had not been keen to explore further. Alfayo was quite organised and full of the word. On that first meeting there were fifteen of them from across their neighbourhood. The singing was amazing with Mimo leading the worship. The songs especially consisted of Swahili hymns and choruses as well as some Christian songs in ethnic languages. Pastor Noel and Sherry Karo were present and on that day each member made an introduction and brief personal and spiritual history including testimonies of what God had done in their lives. Tom had made delicious snacks with tea and juice served as well.

They chose Thursday afternoon as their time of meeting as they would be fairly free from housework before the busy weekend and their off days mostly on Sundays. Pastor Noel shared a word of encouragement to the group. This opened up a discussion of many challenges that arise in their lives and occupation and the discussion suddenly extended into the late evening as one person shared an experience they were going through and yet another shared a similar experience to the one being narrated that they had managed to overcome.

"For me, I would rather engage in something like sewing, listening to music or my new audio Bible than engage in idle gossip about my employers," Eusebia advised.

"I used to prefer staying indoors or outside the compound as well and engage in something useful until my Madam's husband lost his job and started spending too much time in the house when everyone was gone. Eventually, he began making sexual advances at me and so I resorted to going out to chat with others, usually trying my best to limit the conversation to my life and not my boss' family. This helped me avoid too many hours in the house alone with him until I found another job," Mimo said.

"Oh, that's good. One should also watch out what attire to wear when at work. You girls should learn to wear modest dresses and then when you are off duty, you may wear more fashionable clothes," Eusebia added.

"1 Timothy chapter 6 verses 1 and 2 are very useful in guiding one's conduct at work," Alfayo advised and went on to read the verses out loud:

"All you Christians who are servants must respect your owners and work hard for them. Do not let the name of God and our teaching be spoken against because of poor work. Those who have Christian owners must respect their owners because they are Christian brothers. They should work hard for them because much Christian brothers are being helped by their work. Teach and preach these things."

Eventually, after the warm conversation, encouragement and prayer, they left Pastor Noel's house at 7pm.

Chapter 8

❀

"Religion and specifically prayer is a product with numerous consumers. I will turn this old activity into a commodity!" Francis said aloud and quickly looked around. *Of course nobody heard me. I am in my office!* he thought. As he counted the five thousand shillings in cash, he blessed the day he had made that particular realisation and resolution. He also blessed the day he had started his church, the Assembly of Wonders and End Day Miracles. His empire was worth millions of shillings and he commanded quite a bit of respect in some sections of society. His target prey was not the many that despised religion and viewed its adherents as a desperate lot but rather those who were genuine yet ignorant seekers and those who had an interest in Christianity, but for the wrong reasons. *Just as prayer is the medium to reach God, money is the medium of exchange for material valuables in life*, he recited in his mind.

Though she had completed her secondary school education with good grades, Teresa had missed the cut off mark to proceed to the university. Hers had been the case of too much responsibility as a first born girl in a fairly large household combined with the task of studying. She often thought that she would have probably attained the mark and made it to university, had she been at boarding school. Teresa worked as a house help when she initially came to the capital city and then she acquired a job in a cyber cafe. Later, after undergoing some typing and administrative training, she landed a job as a receptionist. As her work and training evolved, she became a front office manager. Teresa was quite happy about how her life had turned out and she felt the need to always remain grateful.

Assembly of Wonders and End Day Miracles congregation was interspersed with an array of actors situated in different parts of the assembly hall. Whenever Apostle Francis declared that the spirit is moving and that those in need of salvation should come to the front, strategic people would pioneer the response by standing up and answering to the altar call. This action would encourage the shy ones to go to the front.

Whenever it was declared that the sick should come to the front in order to be healed, those with ailments went up to the front and these strategic people would also rise up and limp to the front or engage in a dramatic twist, beguiling those present and suddenly they would declare their healing. Others would testify on how their lives had improved since they joined the Assembly of Wonders and End Day Miracles.

A friend had invited Teresa into the church with glowing recommendation of the pastor, Apostle Francis. Teresa had attended the services, which were quite loud, once or twice. She didn't quite feel comfortable with the flamboyant nature of the pastor. The sermons were quite simplistic in nature. They would not centre on doctrinal teachings but rather the physical, financial, emotional needs of the congregation and the need for a miracle for each one as well as exorcisms.

However, initially; she couldn't quite place her finger on what else might be wrong.

Teresa had come to the conclusion that when it came to religious deception from a traditional African context, it is usually a question of science versus magic and marks out the difference on how the religious person of traditional African origin is deceived. Such deception is especially appealing to the quota of individuals who find learning an unnecessary burden and prefer the simplest means of achieving any goal, especially short-cuts.

The nature of formal learning embodies alphabets, methods, formulas and systems. As this learning grows, the learner comes to an understanding of cause and effect, knowing that nothing just happens. Before there is rainfall, evaporation, which is an invisible process, has occurred, forming clouds and producing rain.

As this man observes the wonder of the rising sun, he understands that the sun belongs to the solar system. The learned man understands that there are sound practices in manufacturing any kind of product, as well as methods and strategies of success or failure in a given market. Ultimately, the scientist understands that he must experiment and thereafter come up with solutions. Inevitably, the world keeps turning, sustained by knowledge and improvisation. The creator must have placed these systems and laws in place and a person who is seeking success in their life and believes in God must also believe in the set processes existent in succeeding in whatever discipline, no matter how simple or complex it may be.

Teresa felt that the Bible too needs to be studied and the lessons therein internalised. This study will enable one to distinguish the acceptable interpretations from the

112

unacceptable. Learning and wisdom is emphasised in the book of proverbs. When one is reconciled to cause and effect, consequently, they can understand that it is impossible to be a computer scientist when one has no understanding of how computers work just as it is impossible to be an overnight millionaire unless it is the culmination of previous effort made, winning a lottery or access to an inheritance. Teresa felt a deep anger at what was happening right before her eyes as Apostle Francis spoke and though she had no intention of becoming a pastor, Teresa resolved to attend evening classes at a reputable Bible school and add to her knowledge.

Apostle Francis understood the law of cause and effect well and he marvelled at how gullible his congregation could be, especially in matters that had to do with obtaining material riches. He marvelled at how ignorant members in his congregation believed his every word and gimmick. He was equally surprised at how some who were more learned would fail to employ the very tools of learning by reading their Bibles and practising the Christian faith disciplines thereby finding out who God was for themselves. Consequently they too would be duped. Many preferred the easy way out of unjustified life circumstances like poverty and not a systematic approach. He had come to understand that the traditional African's view towards things progressive was quasi-magical. Technology had brought about electricity, brick and stone houses, running water, not to mention cookers, television sets, all manner of electronics as well as cars and even planes. The traditional definition of prosperity as simply being in possession of a large herd of cattle, many wives and sometimes a large piece of land was no longer in vogue in the developing African setting. Formal education had brought with it different keys to prosperity and with it talent had also come to the fore as a possible vehicle to riches. The essence of literacy, one would think, was to continuously gain access to knowledge whether one attained higher education or not. *However, learning is quite an unnecessary burden to most,* Apostle Francis thought to himself. Some of those who had no access to formal learning due to poverty or culture and whose lives were based in the village viewed modern advancement not as a result of knowledge or process but as magic. Similarly, it was common even for those with an education and an understanding of the working of things to visit the village witchdoctor or *shaman* in order to seek the quick way to advancement.

Initially, Apostle Francis had underestimated how much need flooded the lives of men. He was getting busier and busier as days went by. If it wasn't a suffering wife seeking help for her promiscuous and irresponsible husband to change his behaviour, it would be a teenage girl needing direction. If it wasn't a husband without the means to meet his family's needs, it would be a single lady in her thirties, desperate for a mate. Sometimes it would be an alcoholic wanting to get free of the dreadful habit.

Some situations were scary when entire households would claim to be haunted by some spirit or some who would stretch their imagination with the thought that they could be healed from terminal diseases. *The world sure is a desperate place,* Apostle Francis thought. Week after week different members of his congregation and sometimes total strangers would come into his office and lay their lives bare, like an open book before him. *All one needs is to announce that they have the answer to the world's problems and scores will come pouring,* he mused. Francis often thought himself quite talented; if he would have had the chance to complete his education he sure would have become a somebody. He would make quite a good shrink, he thought. He hated to remember his background which he found pathetic.

They lived in a mud hut and his father was an alcoholic. He was the last born in a family of five sons and two daughters born to his mother who was a very religious woman. They had struggled to go to school with only three of his siblings making it to form four level: two of his older brothers and one sister. Two other brothers had completed their class eight exams but there were no school fees to continue. He had reached class seven.

Apostle Francis had seen it all: desperation, tears, pain, shrieks, screams, hopelessness, wickedness, disease, poverty, plain madness and vacant eyes. How sordid the human condition was! He had also seen health, beauty, eminence, learning, wealth, happiness, talent, strength, love, fortitude and devotion.

There were those who through learning, business, talent, luck or inheritance had advanced and gained most of what anyone would want from this life. These were there but there were also those who desired these same things and had gained them in a different way. After all, many times, there are several routes to a particular destination. And he had managed to get away with much.

As he walked into his office, he encountered a woman. Her back was turned back towards the door when he came in. He walked in and round to his desk.

"How are you mama?" he asked.

"I am well," she answered.

"What might be the problem? You don't look okay. Are the children okay?"

"I don't know what to do Pastor. This man, his name is Paul, has cheated me," Salome began. "He does not want to marry me and I discovered he has a wife. He hasn't offered to do anything for me or my children and to date I have only enjoyed 100 shillings from him. I slept with him. As you know, I live in a single room with my children. This has been happening when they leave for school. But I want God to forgive me. He is a useless guy," she concluded, bowing her head in shame.

Salome was a single mother of four children, two were teenagers and two were still in primary school. Apostle Francis had counselled her on similar issues, a couple of times. *The wonder of folly*, he thought to himself, as he began to speak. "Salome, you claim to love God and then you go out and sleep with different men who have not made any public commitment to you or proposed marriage. You have come to me two times already, lamenting the problems that you have experienced when you last got into such a situation. How do you expect me to help you when you lack the common sense to live as a virtuous single woman in the society; putting the best interests of your children before anything else, even your desire for a man? God will forgive you but don't you ever come to my office with such an issue again," he said looking annoyed.

"Let us pray," he said. They bowed their heads in prayer. "Father forgive this woman for her continuous sinning and folly and help her to follow you," he said.

She handed him an envelope with a 500 shilling note inside and left his office with her head bowed. He opened the envelope and placed the money in his drawer. *"What an idiot!"*

116

he said to himself, half amused and half annoyed. *"Who could tell that a simple, illiterate peasant woman like this can actually pass for a sex addict of sorts?"*

In his self-righteousness, Apostle Francis was quite unsympathetic, especially of women who seemed unable to maintain sexual chastity. Although he too slept with some women other than his wife, he despised them afterwards. As they had grown up, he had seen his mother stick to her virtues through thick and thin, eventually winning his wayward father's confidence too. As the children had grown, his father had slowly changed his conduct and though his mother was delighted, Apostle Francis just didn't care. *Men are a burdened lot, the weight of societal expectations drives some crazy*, he had concluded.

Apostle Francis had a wealthy relative, Jabali More, a cousin to his father who was a businessman. Francis father had unsuccessfully tried to beg his uncle for school fees when he faced his plight back then. He had made the trip with his father. However, the reception Jabali More gave them made Francis despise poverty. Despite having been informed that *Mzee* Katana and his son had come to see him, Jabali More had spent one hour upstairs in his room, only to come down in a rush and upon seeing Francis and his father, he ordered the cook to serve them a meal in the kitchen. Francis father had begged his attention but Jabali said that he had to leave right away in order to catch a flight and with that he got into his car and sped off. The cook in the kitchen had consoled Francis and his father and offered them one thousand shillings for their fare back home. He would replace it from the household expenses. Francis had hated the sight of his father on his knees. In the depths of his heart, he vowed that at whatever cost, poverty was the one thing he would not endure in this life.

*****

Salome left Apostle Francis' office covered in shame. She considered herself an idiot indeed. Her lack of patience was always her undoing. Self-control eluded her many times. She wished there would be a way to have all her burdens lifted from her. Having enjoyed a marriage before being widowed, she often felt desperate. Moving from one church to another without immediate success, she had landed at Apostle Francis' church and somehow it seemed then that life's problems weren't that complex after all; it wasn't that necessary to keep praying like your life depended on it, to fast or to follow the commandments to the letter. She, of course, knew the Ten Commandments even though she was illiterate. She knew that much.

On this day, Salome realised that not even Apostle Francis could help her. She had given away the last 500 shillings she had to a man who had fallen short of insulting her. A man who had no power to help her change or find a lasting, godly mate. Did God really despise her as much as he had made it sound? She was overpowered with the sting of the shame of her fornication as well as her biting poverty and desperation.

"This is the last time I am coming here," she said to herself with tears falling down her face and dry cracked lips.

"*Nisaidie maji ya kunywa*, may I have some drinking water?" she asked the receptionist as she walked out. From the corner of her eyes, through a glistening tear, she could see Samba, the area Member of Parliament seated but was too ashamed to say hello. She hurriedly gulped down the glass of water and walked out of the office. Samba too felt uneasy. Hitherto, he had been accustomed to have Apostle Francis come to his home but today he had insisted that he come to the office.

*****

At exactly 12:00pm Samba had arrived at the church office. He was a practical guy with a political experience. He hailed from a family of political leaders and had enjoyed ten years of a successful political career. This was until his nightmare began in the form of two young activists.

"Yes, they are brilliant fellows and have been drawing some attention to themselves lately, Samba thought, *"How dare they, such poor bastards at best... trying to challenge not only my career but my family and societal prestige. I despise them. People who neither have claim to a name nor property but can only boast of the clothes on their backs and their miserable families living in a one-roomed apartment."*

For the good things he had in his life, Samba had drawn from his family name and prestige almost every time. He was average in school but had a knack for business. His father's name – Jabali More – was legendary. Samba was now in his early fifties, and understood the language of money and power. Jabali More had been brought up by both his parents until he was 17 years of age, when his father died. His father was a settler of Portuguese and British descent. After his death, his mother who was a literate woman had ensured that they went to school and administered the property left in her name by their father.

Apostle Francis grinned as Samba went into his office. He carried his briefcase which contained one million shillings in cash. Samba and Apostle Francis had known each other since they were children. It was Samba's father who had declined to assist Apostle Francis father with school fees to enable the Apostle continue with his education several years ago. The two had played together in the village briefly when Samba as a child would be taken home to visit his grandparents. When he went back to the city though, he forgot about the folks in the rural area. After completing his secondary school, for many years, he hardly went to their rural home since he had travelled to the United States for university studies and had eventually been there for about seven years.

Samba looked around at Apostle Francis' plush office. Frankly, he was quite surprised how this struggling obscure businessman had become quite a religious figure in the last five years. He wondered too at how his church could make him rich. However, considering that he himself was carrying a sum of one million shillings to hand to him without a guarantee that everything he wanted would go smoothly was evidence enough that there was easy cash to be made in this world and religion was such an avenue that granted those who were willing access.

Samba's family name was fast getting into political and moral disrepute with a string of corrupt deals through government resources, entered into by his father and about two which he himself bore responsibility for. The country had changed in the last two decades and today he, Samba More, could find himself at the mercy of civil society groups and activists who held sway on the populace. On the other hand, his old father was keen that Samba must succeed him in his political career, something that he was not keen to do but which he felt compelled to for his father and his wider family's sake.

Apostle Francis looked at Samba and placed the money into his safe. *Who would have thought that Samba would be the one seeking my help in his hour of need?* he thought.

"So tell me Samba, how are you and what do you want me to pray for? The Lord is able to do anything," he said. For a moment, Samba looked at Francis sceptically; he nevertheless bowed down his head in prayer.

*****

Jabali More was aware that the country which he thought he knew was changing rapidly. Human rights were getting more attention than he thought possible and this had emboldened any Tom, Dick or Harry. The activists who were steadily bringing undue unpopular attention to Samba's political career at such a crucial time worried him. Though the young men spoke of corruption in the issuing of tenders and lost public money during Samba's last appointment as a cabinet minister, Jabali knew that they would find more dirt to expose about the More's if they dug a little deeper. According to him, they had to be stopped.

At exactly 11pm, Jabali More left the house. He had informed his driver that he would be working late on this particular day. He got into the back of the vehicle, one of his older cars which he didn't use often. "*Twende* Blackjax Club Westlands, Let's go to Blackjax Club Westlands," Jabali instructed his driver. Without saying a word, the driver switched on the engine and drove out of the compound and onto the road. They reached the club at 11:20pm and Jabali went in and immediately spotted two men, Ninja and Terminator, in a corner table. He went and sat with them as the waiter drew near to ask him what he would like to drink.

121

The men were smartly dressed but nevertheless, appeared to be rather hardened and street smart unlike the rest of the patrons who were mostly young men and women who were well to do and a few older men like Jabali. Jabali ordered a bottle of whisky and lime water. As the waiter served him, Jabali got down to business.

"Ninja and Terminator! Long time my boys," he said grinning.

"Yes indeed boss," they replied.

"I have quite a job for you this time," he said.

"Just let us know what you want Sir," the pair answered.

"There are two activists who are causing a lot of trouble for me and my son Samba. They are doing this at such a crucial time and though their allegations are lies, the whole country will believe them before we get a chance to prove Samba's innocence," he began. "I am sure you have been watching the news and reading the papers haven't you?"

"Yes Sir, Samba is in trouble," Terminator stated.

"This means you also know the two activists who are working with the media to bring us down," he added.

"Yuh!" Ninja said brusquely.

"I want you to teach them a lesson that will slow them down and that they will never forget," Jabali said. "Do everything to deface these two. Break all their bones if you must ... but don't kill them, I don't want that on my conscience."

"What's the price?" Ninja asked.

"I have come with two hundred thousand for the two of you to divide among yourselves and will give you another two hundred thousand after the job is done," he answered.

"I am sure we can do that," Ninja said, his face suddenly lighting up. They shook hands and stood up to leave. Once outside, they followed Jabali to his car where he took out an envelope with the names and addresses of the two activists and the money. They stood a few yards from the car and he handed the money and details to them.

"I am sure you can Google and find clearer pictures of the two in case you have forgotten," he added.

"It will be done Sir," Terminator assured him.

Jabali bid them goodbye, got into his car and instructed his driver to drop him home. It was a week later when the headlines showed separate pictures of the two activists badly beaten and admitted in hospital. Several theories including that of robbery and carjacking were fronted. However, a handwritten paper with the names and details of the two activists had been found at the site where one activist had been found bludgeoned. This among other details pointed to a possible revenge or political retaliation act. Since Samba was not the only high political figure cited in various scandals, it was difficult to point at him. The police said they would investigate and find out who the handwriting belonged to.

Exactly five weeks later, the two young men passed within three days of each other and the lax police shelved the investigation until later. It was at this time, that Samba eavesdropped on a conversation Jabali was having at his study.

"I just read the newspapers and the other young man is dead too... Ninja, the deal was not to kill these young men but to teach them a lesson... to slow them down, let their blood be on your own conscience and never call me again," he said, disconnected his phone and threw it on the floor in anger.

123

"Dad, how long has this been the case?" he asked.

"Oh Samba!" Jabali said turning his chair to face the door. "What are you talking about?" he probed.

"How long has it been that we wash our consciences clean by using poor people's blood?" Samba continued.

"My, my, my, there goes my idealistic oversensitive son again... I always said that you shouldn't join politics if you don't have the mettle son," he said.

Samba collapsed into the seat opposite his father. Suddenly he found the full realisation of his father's character impossible to stomach.

"Although you are trying to pretend that you have no part in this, it is your faults I was trying to cover. I did not instruct for those young men to be killed, I just ordered that they be taught a lesson so that you can have a chance to make something of yourself in this country," Jabali stated. "Samba by now, you have enjoyed everything that money, status and power can buy and instead of trying to dissociate yourself with it, you should be grateful," he said and walked out.

Samba sat in that study for a few minutes and walked out to his car ignoring the cook walking towards him with some juice to drink. He drove straight to his house and slipped into his study. He reflected on the day's events. He had just bribed a pastor he barely trusted one million shillings for prayers to get him ahead in his political career. He had also found out that his father was an accomplice in two murders. He had always known that his father was not necessarily a clean man; he had bribed and harmed others. At the back of his mind, he always knew that the wealth in their family did not all come through hard work and clean hands. However, he did not believe that

124

his father could be absolutely ruthless. He had ignored any rumour he had heard implicating him as causing bodily harm or being an accomplice in anyone's murder.

In retrospect, I think I was just protecting myself from reality for all these years, he thought.

He looked around at his study. There was a picture of his wife and their two children on his desk. Besides this, there was a painting by Sherry Karo on the wall and the picture of eight of them - himself and Natasha, Noel and Sherry, Sheba and Eric Michael and George - on a separate part of the study. This was taken recently when his wife Natasha had insisted that they should attend a marriage enrichment seminar held by the church. For some reason, he loved the picture and had decided to frame it and set it up in his study. The books on his shelf mainly consisted of Business, Economics and Literature. He had some inspirational books mainly bought by his wife. While he had done many things in his life, he had done nothing vile in his own study, as he had just witnessed his father admit to. *I am not my father, I am Samba*, he said. Many times his wife had told him so and many times he had told himself.

A card decorated with the words "New Beginnings" at the far end of his desk seemed to shout at him.

Chapter 9

✳

It was forty-four years since she had been born, and so she had found herself in this world. Eric had held a dinner party to celebrate her birthday and yet all that she could think of was that she was childless. She needed to free herself from all these tags and tugs on her person. A Kenyan, from the Maasai tribe and specifically of the Ole Koina family and lineage, complete with a clan. The Maasai tribe is famous worldwide for their strong adherence to their unique culture. All these forms of identification were good, giving one a sense of history, culture and belonging except when they threatened to undermine the essence and authenticity of one as a human being just as she was, simply, Sheba Shilishoi Mureithi.

There were tugs that pulled her to observe certain customs not as a matter of choice but as a prerequisite to prove that she was indeed a true tribeswoman. It isn't easy for one to break away from a bloodline, a series of generations steeped in rituals, habits, norms and mores, even physical attributes. During their times, it hadn't been easy for her grandparents to break the norm of deciding to acquire formal knowledge and yet today it was rare that a parent should deny their child an opportunity to join school and gain an education. Recently, Sheba had come to the knowledge that her middle name - Shilishoi - was also the name of her late great grandmother. Though she had raised seven children, her great grandmother had been the biological mother of none. Having been widowed after ten years of marriage, her great grandmother found herself childless and alone. She returned to her parent's home. Most people in her community considered her a bad omen since she had been unable to bear any children and worse, had become a widow. Her father and mother in-law especially grieved at the fact that their son had died without a grandson to succeed him and continue with his lineage. Her parents were therefore surprised as was everyone in the village when a suitor, a young widower named Melian, knocked at their door and asked for their daughter's hand in marriage; a daughter who was almost an outcast, having returned to her parents' house after a failed marriage. However, great grandmother Shilishoi was a beautiful and kind woman and Melian, her second husband, loved her deeply and understood her grief, being a widower himself. His late wife had borne him seven children, who were all still young.

Sheba's grandparents had been brought up within this marriage union that had broken the norms in many ways. The villagers would wait for a calamity to occur in the Melian family but instead the children grew up well. It was even more shocking to the villagers that Shilishoi and her husband took the children to the church and mission school where they acquired some formal education, altering their perspective towards life all the more. However, these children, who were her grandparents that bore her parents in turn, had taught their offspring to quit basing their lives on superstition and pursue an excellent life instead and to have faith in God. Lately, the fact that Sheba Shilishoi was childless was attributed to the fact that she was named after a childless woman, who though deeply loved by her husband could not bear him any more children. And just like her, Sheba who had a wonderful husband who

127

adored her could not bear children. Sheba detested the parallel that was being drawn against her situation. What had she to do with an obscure ancestor anyway? Nevertheless, the whispering voices were beginning to cause distress and disturb her peace.

*****

Was it true what a guest pastor who had visited their church had claimed; that there were voices that spoke from one's genealogy disrupting one's present life when one had decided to follow God as described in the Bible as opposed to the traditional deities and ways of worship? *Whatever the case, the voices had to be silenced*, she thought.

Africans had in the past believed in appeasing their ancestors in order to ensure that their lives ran smoothly, devoid of misfortune. Deviating from these fixed cultural practices and rites, it was believed, would lead to dire consequences. However, some who did deviate suffered and others who deviated never quite suffered the consequences spoken of. Only fifty years ago, these practices were very much alive. Presently, some people still clung to them. *If our ancestors believed they had a right to set up this dark heritage that enslaves then we too have a right to decide which way we will go henceforth. I have a right to decide what my life should be and what it shouldn't*, she thought. *Individual conscience and belief is of great value*, Sheba had concluded.

She resorted to a time of prayer and fasting. Taking a week off from her home, she checked into a retreat centre at the outskirts of the city and there she prayed and abstained from food, save for a cup of hot chocolate without milk in the evenings. Her husband was away on a trip and it was therefore the perfect time for her to devote some time to prayer.

Sell Me a Prayer

What does one do with an unscheduled morning? Sheba thought after completing one hour in prayer and another thirty minutes reading the Bible. The retreat centre held a service each day in the evenings for those who had come in for prayer. Since the day was still ahead, she resolved to enjoy her time of solitude until that time came. She took a shawl and went outside to savour the beautiful surrounding garden and sunshine while reading a book she had bought and meditating. She said hello to a few other people on her way to the gardens as they also went about their business. At 1pm Sheba went into a prayer room that was available and there she prayed her heart out. She cried and felt a weight lifted from her shoulders, reciting the scriptures filled with God's promises.

In the afternoon she prayed about her name and every wrong thing there may have been in the life of the person she was named after. Shilishoi had the implied meaning of "one whom people came to see" and implies a child who brought in visitors to celebrate in amazement. She had resolved not to change her name since it had a beautiful meaning but nevertheless, to refuse any unholy connection with the circumstances of the particular woman - her great grandmother Shilishoi - whom she was named after and who might not have even had a clue of what was besetting her life more than hundred years ago.

Sheba had spent that week in drawn out sessions of prayer, silence, meeting new friends and daily evening chapel services with the other attendees. When the week came to a close, she left with a deep peace and knowledge that God would do what is best in her life. She felt as if she was riding on the strength of another and she felt a deep joy. *This must be what is really referred to as grace*, she thought.

At the close of the week she packed her belongings and bidding her new friends goodbye She got into her car and left. Just as she drove outside the gate of the retreat centre she noticed a familiar looking car driving towards the retreat centre. It was Mrs Natasha More's car. However, as the vehicle approached, she could tell that it wasn't Mrs More in the car. It was her husband Samba!

They both stopped their vehicles and Sheba got out and shook Samba's hand.

"Hello More, how are you?"

"I am very well my dear," Samba replied.

"I actually thought it was Natasha coming when I saw her car," Sheba continued.

"I thought I should borrow a leaf from her this time. I am the one in need of reflection Sheba. How is Eric doing?" he inquired.

"He is doing okay, he is back at work, this time ensuring that the systems at the warehouse are working well," she answered. "And how is Natasha?"

"Natasha is doing okay, she needed to use a four wheel vehicle because we are having visitors from abroad and she is taking them to Maasai Mara for a visit and so she borrowed both my car and driver."

"Very well, let me leave you to it. "I am starving, as you can imagine," she said jokingly. Samba laughed in his jolly characteristic manner as he drove on to the retreat centre.

As he was welcomed to the retreat centre, Samba wished he didn't attract as much attention. Everybody at the lobby looked up in recognition when the secretary mentioned his name. Samba bore a name that many would have liked to identify with. With this name came the burden of continuing a legacy. A legacy he did not care about. Samba recalled the tale of trees in a forest which his grandmother had narrated to him.

There was once a forest whose name was Strong. The trees in this forest took root and quickly flourished. There was a wide variety of tree species arranged in clusters. Some of the older trees were a hundred years old. They had flourished in this soil. Usually, when a tree was old and gnarled and had reached the end of its lifespan, it would fall on the floor of the forest where it may be collected for some other useful work. As one tree fell, there would be young tree seedlings sprouting up and growing on the floor of the forest, nourished by that soil that had held upright thousands of trees before.

The years wore on; Happy, a young tree of about fifty years old cherished the forest and spread her branches out wide with new foliage, thankful for the forest floor and its nourishing soil.

Lately, however, her part of the forest felt empty and scary. One by one, in the span of two years, two dozen trees in her cluster of species had fallen at different times. Many times, there had been no sign whenever a tree fell. A number of the fallen trees were deemed the best in the forest with beautiful foliage and strong, thick stems. There were instances when a tree's leaves would be infected with disease which would linger and deteriorate as the tree fell. The mystery in the tale of the trees baffled many. However, Happy was a keen observer of life. She noticed what seemed to be a thread of coincidence among the exposed roots of the fallen trees. Their roots were diseased and rotten. Upon observing the roots, it was evident that though the signs of a dead, diseased tree did not always show on the foliage, it had only been a matter of time.

As each tree fell, Happy was left wondering what caused the disease. The soil was fertile, she thought, at least it had nourished strong trees which lived a hundred years or more.

She decided to go on a quest. Had the trees changed or had the soil changed? She went around asking this question. The other trees who weren't affected mostly shrugged off the question while those from her species were equally perplexed. As she continued to inquire, Mythola, an old tree which was ninety years old, was willing to answer Happy.

"In the last fifty years," Mythola said, "the trees seem to grow faster than they did before. I know that our soil has not changed for sure but the trees have changed. Their leaves are bigger, their height a little taller and their branches wider. Unfortunately, with these changes, a shorter lifespan has resulted. A solution would only be realised if the problem was solved by examining the root... Solutions in life can only be attained when one digs into their root."

Samba felt that this time he would spend away from the public in prayer and contemplation would expose the root problem in his life.

*****

George looked at Michael as he lay asleep on their bed. Something about them had changed. She wondered if he may have been having an affair with another woman. Previously, he had been liberal enough to disclose information on where he would be at any given time but lately he would arrive in the dead of the night and would not conclusively explain where he had been.

That seemed to be a lesser problem for George though. In a span of two months, she had experienced terrible nightmares, especially when Michael was away. She would speak to him about it but he would brush it off, asking her to say a prayer.

"What have you been watching on television honey? I understand those Nigerian movies can be scary!" he once joked.

"Michael you are well aware that Eusebia is the champion when it comes to watching Nigerian movies and even when I do, we sift them carefully and don't entertain the weird stuff," she answered.

The most troubling aspect of the dream was that Michael seemed to be featuring in quite a number of them. At one time, she dreamed that she and Michael were standing side to side when suddenly the ground cracked separating the two of them. She had started screaming as Michael was drifting further and further away. The strange part of the dream was that Michael was in fact oblivious of the situation. Eventually, a monster or demon of sorts appeared and grabbed Michael, throwing him into the chasm that had formed between them and separated them. She would try to call for help but there seemed to be nobody in sight.

She had had the same dream about one week later, but this time, Michael was carrying their little girl Cherie when it all happened and both he and Cherie had been thrown into the chasm.

She would wake up with a splitting headache and great thirst. After these dreams, George would get on her knees and pray fervent and desperate prayers against whatever evil was meant in the dream. She especially asked for protection for her entire family, especially her husband. She increasingly felt fearful and didn't know how to share with anyone yet.

One day as she was sleeping, she suddenly saw Michael's face and watched in horror as his handsome features suddenly contorted and turned monstrous and ugly. "He is mine!" an ugly voice said. Suddenly, George woke up with a scream so loud and piercing.

Eusebia sat up on her bed. Had she been dreaming or had she heard a scream? As she wondered, she heard the word Jesus! She was certain that that had been George's voice. *Sir Michael is away, but why is George screaming?* she asked herself. Grabbing hold of her phone, she scrolled to her boss' number and called her.

The sound of the phone ringing sent another faint scream out of George's throat and she grabbed the phone by the bedside lamp.

"Madam George, is everything okay, *nishi?* What is it?" Eusebia asked.

"Eusebia, *njoo tafadhali, hamba,* Please come!" she said.

Eusebia put on a large oversized sweater and left her house which was a few yards behind the main house where George was. Her sitting room window was adjacent to George and Michael's bedroom window upstairs.

There was pin drop silence as it usually is at night when suddenly George heard the sound of crying. It was her little girl, Cherie. She switched on the light and went to her bedroom.

"Mommy!" Cherie said. George held her and after a few minutes, she calmed down and rolled over asleep.

Outside Eusebia was met by the night guard Amos who was similarly concerned about what could be happening in the house to cause George to scream as she had. Michael certainly *isn't in, is he?* Amos thought. *And even if he is, is he giving his wife a beating or what?*

"Where are you going?" he asked Eusebia as she walked onto the yard.

"I am going to check on Mrs George," she answered as Amos struggled to hold the two dogs on guard on their leashes.

George opened the front door and Eusebia got into the house. She went to the kitchen and boiled some water. She picked up George's green tea and set it on the table serving her. George had done the same thing for her when she was sick with worry about her child Rose and her sickness.

"Eusebia, I have had some terrible dreams in the past month and a half," George said feverishly. She was shivering as she sipped the tea.

"Last week, I dreamed that a large snake was swallowing up my husband Michael as I stood by and it was terrifying and I didn't know what to do. I prayed a lot and felt some relief. I had a fast last Wednesday. Can you remember?"

"Yes, I can remember very well," Eusebia answered.

George switched to mother tongue and explained to Eusebia what she had been encountering, narrating the dreams to her. Eusebia sat calmly and listened. She too had had two bad dreams of her own. One had to do with a night when she had a dream that a dark cloud was coming towards the house and was trying to envelop the bright sunny blue sky above them. The second one was worse since it had to do with their being in a funeral where they were burying Sir Michael and little Cherie. She told the two dreams to George.

"You know what George," Eusebia said. "If we pray together, God will hear us. He has promised to protect us. I

135

can never forget what he did for my daughter Rose, you know. Let's pray for about an hour pleading with God and speaking his protection and preservation upon Sir Michael, Cherie and all of us. Let us ask him to take away the cloud of darkness that wants to cover this house."

"You're right, Eusebia," George answered suddenly gaining courage. *It feels good to have someone with a sound mind around me at this time,* she thought.

They began to pray together and about forty-five minutes later, George began to feel a difference in the air. Five minutes later, they had concluded praying. The clock struck 4:00am. They had started talking at about 1:00 am and began praying 2 hours later.

Eusebia retreated to her quarters and George went to sleep, she felt more peaceful. She slept soundly waking up at 7:00am, feeling refreshed. Eusebia had already woken up at 6:00am, thirty minutes later than her usual time of 5:30am. She had made breakfast and prepared Cherie for school. Eusebia had drawn the curtains and golden streams of tropical sunshine streamed into the house. Suddenly George felt that life was okay after all and everything would go on smoothly. That day as she left the house for work, she was thankful to have someone like Eusebia for a house help.

When Sunday came, Eusebia went for the first service which was in Swahili as she usually did. However, she didn't proceed to wherever she wanted. She came back, prepared breakfast and got Cherie ready for church. Usually, she would go for the early Swahili service and proceed to visit relatives and friends as Sunday was her day off. However, this Sunday she did not do that, sensing that perhaps George needed her company or help, in case she had visitors in the afternoon.

136

She decided to accompany them back to church for the first English service. *After all, I enjoy those English songs very much,* she said to herself.

Eusebia held Cherie in her arms and nodded pleasantly to the tune that came from the worship team at the pulpit. It was a song by American gospel musician, Don Moen.

> *"You are the one that I love.*
> *Light of the world sent from above*
> *Sing Hallelujah, shout to the Lord*
> *You are the One, you are the one I love ..."*

Sherry Karo played the violin part of the song which Eusebia especially liked. To her, the violin sounded just like the *ishiriri,* a traditional stringed instrument from the Luhya community in Western Kenya, which Eusebia hailed from. The preacher stood to preach and the crux of his message was that there are voices all around us and we can't help but hear.

"There is need to distinguish these voices, identifying the source of each voice. Some voices will speak of danger ahead and a voice may speak of the need to change one's behaviour. Yet another voice may speak to our lower nature, drawing you to sinful acts like adultery, fear, manipulation, insecurity and all manner of evil. In all these things, learn to distinguish the voice of God," he said.

George thought long about these words. She considered what she had been through in the past two months and distinctly felt the voice that her family, especially her husband, was in danger. She felt the need to speak to the Pastor about it. Even though there were other counsellors in the church, she felt the deep need to speak to Pastor Noel about it. After the service was over, she left Eusebia who was holding Cherie's hand, speaking and saying hello to other members and hastened to the church office to book an appointment to see the Pastor on Tuesday the following week. Mary, the church secretary, present as always, was there to make the appointment. Pastor Noel was still inside the auditorium, speaking with congregants.

Later, George joined Eusebia and Cherie, saying hello to old time friends like Sheba, Eric, and Teresa, among others. Eusebia was engaging in a lively chat with Mimo, the young woman who worked for Sheba and Eric. Mimo left shortly after to enjoy the rest of her day off.

*****

On Tuesday morning, Pastor Noel sat behind his desk and read his schedule. He usually tried to stick to his day's plan as much as possible but would also attend to the surprising or urgent matters that cropped up on certain days. This day, Samba More, Salome and George Mumbai were among those who had booked an appointment. *"Mumbai" What a funny name that is!* he thought. George's husband Michael Mumbai had been named after the city where he had been born. His parents had gone to India for studies and married each other there. Samba had decided to pay his friend Pastor Noel a visit and talk him into supporting his bid, or at least to make it appear like he did. Though they weren't very close, their wives were close and they had grown up as family friends As much as he hated his father's methods, he would try and align himself with more preferable people.

Samba entered Pastor Noel's office with a wide smile. "Hey Noel!" he started, "It's been a long time!"

"Yes indeed it has," Pastor Noel replied, smiling back. Samba couldn't help but notice that Noel had lost quite some weight. *At least ten kilos*, he thought. Samba knew that though Pastor Noel was at his lowest point since he knew him, he still had quite some influence in society. He knew that a public endorsement from him as a favourite candidate would do wonders. Already, quite a number of influential pastors had agreed to back him up for public office. In return he had donated sums of money to their personal and church accounts. When it comes to giving money to preachers, you couldn't call it bribery as such, it was a donation and it would cater for the Almighty's interests. Some of these interests included feeding the poor as well as enriching the clergy so that they may be equipped in doing God's work more effectively.

Samba looked at a painting on Pastor Noel Karo's office wall. "What a painting!" he remarked. "Your wife Sherry is still quite an artist.. How much would that painting cost?" he asked.

Noel hesitated.

"Seriously, how much? I would like to buy it and gift it to my wife," he said.

"Well, I don't know and it isn't for sale," Pastor Noel answered.

"Pastor Noel, you have many more paintings because you have Sherry, come on give her a call and ask her how much it would cost if she sold this particular piece. Don't you want to cheer her up a little for her efforts?" he insisted.

Pastor Noel picked up his phone and called Sherry and after a brief conversation, she acceded to the proposal. "Well, Sherry says that she will sell this particular piece at two hundred thousand only," he disclosed.

"Well, two hundred thousand it is then," Samba replied. He reached his inside coat pocket, took out his cheque book, wrote out a cheque for her and handed it to Pastor Noel.

"Well thank you again Samba, I know my wife will feel blessed and rewarded for her artistic gift and work," he concluded as he rose to take down the picture. Picking up the phone, he called in Mary, the church secretary, to arrange for the painting to be wrapped up. He also requested her to bring them some coffee.

They chatted on as Samba waited for the opportune moment to get to the core of his mission to Pastor Noel's office. Samba was used to the best things in life and paying the price to obtain these things as well. If it was travel, it had to be first class airline travel and first class accommodation. He had even managed to acquire excellent education in America as his father had sent him to the best school that could accept his grades. He didn't manage to get into the first class Harvard or Princeton type since very high qualifications would be needed to obtain admission but managed to obtain admission to the best of the second tier universities that he qualified for.

"I can see that you have completed most of the remaining work on the church auditorium Pastor. Congratulations," he said.

"Thank you, Samba. The church members have persevered with us, the leadership, to see its completion," he replied. "This has come at a very high personal cost though, hasn't it? It's the cost of leadership and the sacrifice for what one believes in. We haven't concluded absolutely everything, there are a few touch ups yet to be done as you might have noticed."

"Isn't it wonderful to know that even public figures like politicians can contribute to the building of the temple?"

Samba remarked. "You do know how Herod the Great helped to repair the great Jewish temple and how magnificent he made it!" Samba continued, displaying the little knowledge he had in Bible history.

"Yes, he did help repair the second temple which was often desecrated in the wars before the time of Christ. But you know the only reason that made Herod the Great participate in the repair of the temple was because he was extremely unpopular among the Jews at that time due to his cruelties whose climax was slaughtering of the infant boys born during the time of Christ. He did it in the 18th year of his reign to somewhat gain favour among the Jewish community, about 16 years before Christ. Herod employed 18000 men in this temple, suitable for use in 9 years or about 8 years before Christ. Subsequent additions continued increasing in splendour and magnificence until 64 A.D." Pastor Noel completed the history.

"Indeed!" Samba exclaimed. "Noel, I have something here for you that will boost your endeavours," he said lifting up his briefcase and laying it on his table.

"I have the sum of one million to contribute to the rest of the building project or perhaps to get you a cheap car for your wife," Samba said. "Consider this as my contribution to God's kingdom as Samba and also as the future member of parliament in your area."

Pastor Noel looked at the sum of money before him and felt a great discomfort about it. Yes, he was terribly in need. However, why would Samba want to make a private contribution to the church project? Would it be right for him to accept to buy a car with this money, especially knowing that Samba wasn't a committed Christian, nor was he a regular attendee of the church? Furthermore, it had actually been quite a while since he had come to church. Over one year ago. As Pastor Noel sat silently, with these thoughts running through his mind, Samba considered his proposal a success.

Samba smiled and made a brief call. "Richard, you can come in with the camera," he said.

"You don't mind us taking a picture to commemorate this contribution, do you?" he said to Pastor Noel.

Pastor Noel felt anger rise up within him and Samba suddenly realised that Noel seemed agitated. In a short while, Richard the photographer burst into the office.

"Come on Pastor Noel," Samba urged. However, Noel's mind was now as clear as ever. It had dawned on him that this was a trap. He felt ambushed. Remaining behind his desk, he resorted not to get up from his seat.

"I am sorry, I can't accept the money Samba and I cannot take any picture for now," he said calmly.

"What! Noel, you know me. We have known each other since we were young just as our parents have and now you can't accept any money from me?" Samba said in disbelief and veiled anger.

"I know we have known each other for a long time Samba but I still cannot accept the money. It would be unethical," Noel said firmly. He remained seated.

"Forget about the photograph Richard, please pick up that briefcase and let's go," Samba said.

"So long Noel," Samba said reluctantly.

"So long," Noel answered.

Richard shut the briefcase and picked it up and they left.

*****

George Mumbai had been sitting at the reception area waiting for her turn to get into Pastor Noel's office. Mary, the receptionist glanced at her twice. *George does seem disturbed and weary today. It is quite unlike her,* she thought. George was usually a composed and confident woman and the bizarre occurrences in her life were quite disturbing. Samba nodded at George as he marched out of Pastor Noel's office to the reception area and out.

Pastor Noel took several minutes to compose himself. He said a prayer, renouncing the bribery and bigotry that Samba had tried to entrap him into at his office on that day. He took a glass of juice and within five minutes, he instructed the secretary to let George Mumbai into his office.

George was relieved to finally get into the pastor's office and pour out her heart. As she entered and they exchanged greetings, Pastor Noel noticed that she was not her usual self. George seemed deeply disturbed.

"Would you like some coffee, tea, or juice," he asked her.

"Anything is okay," she answered. Picking up the phone, Noel requested Mary to bring in some orange juice for George. She promptly brought it in as Noel inquired after George's family, her children and her husband and their ever smiling house help Eusebia.

George quickly answered in the affirmative and went on to narrate to Pastor Noel the recent experiences she had had in her family.

"Is Michael back from South Africa yet?" he asked.

"No, he isn't," she answered.

"Well, well," he said. Pastor Noel sat in thought. The situation George had described was a series of warnings allowed by God to George indicating that everything was not alright with her family and that they were in grave danger as far as spiritual matters are concerned. There was need to heed to the warnings by way of prayer, fasting and discernment in order to get to the root of the problem.

"My sister George," he began. "Our world is made of material things but as you well know, having been a Christian for a while; what is unseen is in fact more real than what is seen. The Bible says in Eph. 6:12 *'For we wrestle not against flesh and blood, but against principalities, against powers, against the rulers of the darkness of this world, against spiritual wickedness in high places.'* There is a whole world of unseen spiritual beings both good and evil. Our spiritual disposition affects how we operate in our daily lives, George. For now, I would like to request you and your family members to get into a three-day fasting and prayer period along with two young men - members of our church - who have some experience in dealing with such issues. I will fast with you for the first two days as well but since I need to travel shortly to Mombasa. I will not fast with you for the third day. Since Michael is away as well as your two older children, you may invite your sister Phyllis and Eusebia whom you have told me is in the picture as well and do this together. On the third day, these two young men will come into your home and pray with you for several hours in the night to reverse whatever evil may lie ahead. I don't know the root cause of what you are going through but in due time, it will be revealed. They and you will update me while I am away. However, to begin this whole exercise, I will come with some elders to your home this very evening for prayer."

George felt a sigh of relief. It was wonderful to know that she was not alone in what she was going through. It was comforting to know that the battle against her family can be won. Pastor Noel said a prayer of guidance and protection for her before she left.

"See you at 6pm later today," he said. George left the office encouraged and hastened to return to her home in order to prepare for the pastor and elders' evening call.

*****

Next in was Salome, who had been away from church for quite a while. As she entered Pastor Noel's office, she couldn't help but remember the shameful ordeal she had experienced when she had visited Apostle Francis' office. Her shoes were covered in dust and she looked really tired.

"Praise God. How are you pastor?" she greeted him.

"Amen Salome, how are you today?" Pastor Noel inquired.

Salome bowed her head and answered she was okay. *The sun is really hot outside and she must have been walking for a while, going about her business*, Pastor Noel thought. He then phoned Mary the receptionist and asked her to bring a glass of juice for Salome who looked quite weary. Sabuni was a distance away from the church, about thirty minutes walk and he knew she must have walked.

Mary brought in some juice and cookies into the office and left. Pastor Noel took the liberty to speak with another person on phone as Salome took a few sips of the juice. Salome fidgeted in her chair wondering how to begin the conversation. Pastor Noel sensed her unease.

"How have you been Salome? It has been quite a while since I saw you at church and everybody has missed you," he began.

145

"I am very well Pastor, but I have been going through some very hard times and I have also sinned against the Lord," she replied.

"Are you working now? How are the children?" Pastor Noel nudged.

"The children are fine but my work has been quite bad and also I have been having relationships that don't work," she answered. "Pastor I have been seeking some prayers from Assembly of Wonders and End Day Miracles but the Pastor there insulted me the last time I went there and to make the matters worse I give money all the time but seem to be getting poorer," she added, tears flowing down her cheeks. She took out a handkerchief from her bag and wiped her face.

Pastor Noel counselled her, "Salome let me make it plain that we are born in an imperfect world and into imperfect situations and backgrounds. However, a human being is never born to be discarded, no matter how tough his circumstances or how wicked he has been but rather to be redeemed because of their immeasurable value and yet, when a human being rejects redemption, he at best, has discarded his worth. In this respect, everybody has the ability to begin life on a new page, no matter how ugly the previous one might be."

*****

On reaching her home, George briefed Eusebia on the conversation they had had with the pastor and his instructions concerning the issue at hand. Eusebia who was lately more informed about scripture due to the audio Bible she listened to as well as Bible teachings concurred that what the pastor had instructed was appropriate. He had not tried to extort any money from George in order to help her as he should at this time. George then made a call to her sister who lived about forty-five minutes away, requesting her to come in briefly in the evening as well as to Sheba, one of her best friends. Since Sherry Karo, the Pastor's wife was having guests at her house that week, she did not call her. Her younger sister, who was on leave, agreed to come and by 5pm she was already at George's house where George briefed her on what had happened.

Meanwhile, Andrea the elder and two deacons were available to accompany Pastor Noel to George Mumbai's house for prayer. Sherry Karo also accompanied them; having noticed George hadn't been her usual self lately. At exactly six o'clock they arrived. Eusebia had already prepared refreshments and set them aside in order to be able to participate in the prayer session, at least as much as she could. She was better educated on the Bible and the Christian doctrine but was still largely illiterate and did not fully understand English. However, she was catching an increasing number of words and phrases here and there, having been exposed to the language over a long period working at the Mumbai household.

They sang some worship songs together and already George felt uplifted. Pastor Noel read again from the book of Ephesians and encouraged George to be strong and that God would surely answer their prayer. He told her, "As Christians with a personal relationship with God, you are fighting this battle from a winner's vantage point, going through the motions with courage that God is able."

Elder Andrea also spoke to George and assured her that he had seen other cases of fear and threats from the enemy over the years but the Lord had come through for those particular people and would do the same for her.

They all left and promised to send a team to them after the three days of fasting and consecration. Sherry Karo and George's sister shared some more and had tea with the clergy.

*****

Michael arrived the next week just after they had completed the fast. He was very tired and went to sleep after taking only a glass of juice and some salad. On the next day, he was up early to see Cherie off to school and to give her some toys he had bought for her. Michael dropped Cherie to school when he was around. They had breakfast together and he showed her a few toys as she beamed in sheer delight. On this particular morning, both her mother and Eusebia were nonexistent it seemed as the little girl gave her father full attention and received his attention in equal measure. George breathed a sigh of relief as she savoured a few moments to herself which usually helped her recharge. She was reporting to work by 9am and so she had to get ready to leave as well. The young men who were coming to conduct prayers including an overnight vigil were due to arrive that evening and George needed to inform Michael that they would have visitors with them that evening.

Michael returned to the house, having bought the morning papers and gearing for his coffee and a time of reading and relaxing. He went over to the dining table where the smell of toasted bread, fried eggs and bacon beckoned. A jug of freshly blended mango juice looked quite inviting and he poured some into a glass for himself. He reached out and picked a napkin from a bundle of crisp, white neatly folded table linen in a basket at the corner of the dining area.

George walked by just as he poured himself a cup of coffee and requested that Michael drop her off to work as well. Michael gulped down the coffee and dared not protest knowing full well that if he did it might grow into a full blown fight which was quite unnecessary. *Women. Attention. And yet I have missed this woman. I adore her and though dropping her off will delay my morning read, it is probably well worth it,* he thought.

Michael promptly dropped off George at work and promised to pick her up at 5pm after having picked up their daughter Cherie. He had no other engagements besides meeting a few associates at the country club in the afternoon. He got home to the remainder of his breakfast and spent an hour reading the various dailies. He went into the study and looked to see if there was any new reading material and sure enough, he found a new Bible devotional and studied two pages referring to his Bible which was a little dusty on the shelf, for about thirty minutes. Saying a prayer of thanksgiving for God's protection on his family while he had been away and for protecting him as well, he left the study and went to the garden to spend a few minutes listening to Alfayo the guard and the gardener's chatter as they updated him on all and sundry.

He loved it when they felt free to talk with him and some of the stories they had left him in stitches. For example, there was the story of this drunk and cunning husband called Mbogori who left the farm chores and responsibilities to the wife. The hardworking wife had saved enough and bought the family a dairy cow. The drunkard had an accumulated debt that had come about as a result of his attempting to con someone off their hard earned money, borrowing it as a loan. One evening the lender had threatened him severe consequences if he failed to pay up in 24 hours. Since he had used the money on drinking and women, Mbogori could not ask his wife for assistance. He had searched all her favourite places she used to hide money and found none and had therefore come up with an ingenious plan. He waited until the dead of night and the plan was executed. Two of his associates in the guise of thieves came and stole away the dairy cow to pay off the debt. Mbogori had been drinking and he pretended to be dead drunk and dead asleep as his distressed wife tried to wake him! He woke up an hour after they had left!

*****

At 1pm, Eusebia announced that lunch was ready and Michael hurried off and took a quick shower before having his lunch. He later sat down to eat and left for the country club at exactly 2pm. Michael spoke to his friends while enjoying a beer. He was a social drinker and didn't drink much. They were contemplating to diversify their professional and income portfolios. There was growing need for quality housing in the city and the three gentlemen were contemplating getting into real estate development. Michael was seriously considering taking that direction. His job was quite demanding and he wanted to spend more time with his family members and to get involved in empowering his community through creating jobs and inspiring the young ones and youth through supporting education and mentoring.

As they shared details of a ten acre piece of land on the outskirts, Michael received a phone call. His face slowly became tense as he got off his stool at the bar and stepped a few yards away from his friends. The call came from Cherie's teacher at school informing him that she couldn't reach his wife George and that Cherie was experiencing difficulty in breathing and complained of chest problems. Cherie had suddenly felt asphyxiated and was rushed to the hospital. Michael was beside himself with stress and worry.

He quickly tried to contact George and informed her of what had happened to Cherie. George, who was preparing to conclude the final part of her day quickly, informed the doctor and nurse that she had to leave. *I wish they had brought her here, didn't they know I work here?*

She rushed to the hospital. She had a strange feeling. Though she was used to taking care of patients; it was a totally different feeling when a close member of one's family was involved. She reached the hospital and quickly rushed to where Michael and Cherie were. She found Cherie awake and a little dazed at the doctor's office. The doctor had managed to resuscitate her from the fainting that had resulted from asphyxiation. The doctor had run other routine exercises and asked Michael if Cherie had ever had asthmatic problems and he informed them that Cherie was a perfectly healthy child who rarely visited hospital.

"There's nothing we can identify that caused her asphyxiation and fainting. We will have to discharge her for now and ask you to bring her back in case of anything, okay?" the doctor instructed.

"Okay doctor," Michael answered picking up Cherie and carrying her as they went to the parking lot.

"I came with my car as well, what to do now?" George muttered.

"I am riding with daddy," Cherie's sharp but somewhat weak voice volunteered.

"Oh it's okay honey," George answered, smiling at her. "I'll follow you guys behind." She was relieved that Cherie was alright and scared at the same time since she was already scared about what might happen due to the dreams she had been having. Thankfully, today they would hold a night vigil at the house and pray to the early hours of dawn.

At exactly 6pm, the young men assigned by Pastor Noel to assist George and her family in prayer arrived. She welcomed them and minutes later, as tea was served, Michael began to ask them questions, eager to know their background and their occupation. The two young men were college graduates and had simple jobs. Eugene, one of them, was a mechanic and the other one Simon, was a bus driver. Simon drove long distances for a bus transport company and would get one week off his schedule in a month. The two however, were very zealous and upon entering the living room, they had refused to take a seat or to shake anyone's hand before praying.

Michael was satisfied with the fact that the two young men were not idle people without an income, itinerant prayer merchants who went about offering people prayers and acting desperate. Although he didn't understand too much when it came to deep spiritual matters, Michael trusted that his wife George knew more than enough about "deep spiritual matters".

They had supper at 7:30 pm and at about 8:30pm little Cherie fell asleep and Michael carried her to her bed and tucked her in. Cherie absolutely loved it when her father was around and insisted that he does everything for her during the first two weeks of his return after he had been away for long. George served the young men some tea and began briefing them on the bizarre dreams she had been having and also about the incident Cherie had had at school on that day. They quietly took it all in and inquired for more details.

"What work does your husband do?" one of them inquired humbly. Michael explained to them that he was a pilot with the country's largest airline and had to travel over long periods of time.

At ten o'clock they began by singing worship songs and reading portions of scripture. They then began to pray, asking all present to also engage in prayer for the next thirty minutes or so. However, the session lasted about two hours as they prayed and the young men broke into a worship song here and there in the middle of the prayer session. Michael was keeping pace, though he sat and stood in intervals. At midnight, they began reading scriptures again and one of them began elaborating the scriptures in a thirty minute mini sermon. The mini sermon that was based again on 2 Cor.10:4 which states: "*We use God's mighty weapons, not mere worldly weapons, to knock down the Devil's stronghold*", and Eph.6:12-18.

After this, Eugene and Simon began praying specifically about the occurrences that had been happening in George's life and against any plan of evil against Michael and George's family.

It was at the height of these pronouncements in prayer led by the two young men that Michael suddenly began to react strangely. Michael and Georgina had knelt and Eugene, Simon, Eusebia and George's sister Phyllis stood around them in a circle as they prayed. He screamed and let out some choking sound from his throat and fainted. Simon and Eugene took some water and removed their sweaters which they had hitherto worn. They began to pray and use the name of Jesus Christ. George felt a little paralysed and her lips were dry. She had a dreadful feeling at the pit of her stomach and her heart felt heavy as lead. Nevertheless she stood where she was

153

without much reaction as the young men lifted Michael onto the couch.

"Don't worry Mama Cherie," Eugene said to George. "Everything will be alright."

They continued in prayer for about ten minutes. Though it was cold in the wee hours of the morning, Simon was actually breaking into a sweat. Suddenly Michael opened his eyes and coughed. All was quiet and Phyllis, wanting to be helpful, poured a glass of water and brought it to Michael. However, Simon took the water and placed it aside as he began to interrogate Michael.

"Michael, do you belong to any clubs, groups or societies? Have you joined any religious organisation or society recently?"

Michael, a confident man in most circumstances sat on the couch pale and his eyes full fear. He remained quiet and Eugene repeated the question to him. Simon took the glass of water and gave it to him and urged him to drink, telling him that all would be well. Michael took a few sips of the water and sat, stiff on the couch.

After another quiet moment, he spoke. "I joined a society, a society that consists of all religions and whose members are men only. A colleague introduced me to the society and I have met a lot of prominent people at the three meetings I have attended so far," he said quietly.

George began to cry when he mentioned the name of the society since she knew that it was camouflaged as a decent society but yet it was in actual fact an occultist organisation that targeted prominent men and those with strong potential as well and it was present in almost all countries in the world.

"Don't cry Mama Cherie, this is not the time for crying. When it is time for war, we fight and not cry," Eugene said as Phyllis handed George a Kleenex tissue and held her hand.

"I have been having very bad dreams myself," Michael blurted out, "and I wasn't sure what the connection was. I haven't yet fully agreed to join the society. I just wanted to attend a few meetings first."

"When we came here we already had a clue about the problem but not full information. This is because we have been praying and fasting together with your wife, Eusebia and Phyllis about this situation. However, it was hidden since you hadn't told your wife about the society and asked her of her opinion before joining. You didn't ask your pastor Noel either," Simon stated.

"It is prudent for you to have found out more about this group of people Michael because your whole family has been endangered by your move. It is common knowledge to most serious Christians that that society is not what they purport to be, even though they have appeared to be more open to the larger society, even participating in blood donation drives and charity events. This is a society whose members seem to prosper materially, yet they end up having strange deaths in their families and all manner of manifestations. Are you ready to renounce your connection with them for now and the future through Jesus Christ?" Eugene asked.

Michael was shaking as he said a weak "Yes."

They once again asked him to kneel and led him through a prayer renouncing all connection with the said society and its representatives. After about an hour, calm settled in the atmosphere of the house and then Eugene told Michael and George that it would be well and no harm would come towards them from that source. It was 5 am in the morning and everyone felt like they had been doing the hardest form of physical labour for hours on end. They said final prayers of dedicating the house and family members to God through Jesus Christ. Eusebia had disappeared into the kitchen and at this juncture, she emerged with a tray of tea and biscuits for those present.

They took tea mostly in silence as Phyllis had put on some Christian music. At 6pm, everyone was shown where they could lay down and take a rest for a few hours as the day crept in.

It was not until 11 am when everybody was awake and after they had taken breakfast - prepared by Eusebia with Cherie's help - they showered and gathered at the living room. Cherie who was unaware of the occurrences that took place at night was fresh and bright, infusing an atmosphere of cheer to the house.

Eugene and Simon urged especially Michael to join prayer classes at Woodlands City Congregation in order to empower himself more and to know the connection between the Bible and prayer. After a short prayer and a thank you from George and Michael - who looked much better than the previous night - they left.

When the children came home for the holidays, George and Michael, with the help of Pastor Noel, narrated to them what had happened in a way they could understand. It would take months of serious prayer and counselling for George and her family to overcome the fear that had gripped them during their just ended period of difficulty.

Chapter 10

"Our Father who is in heaven,
Hallowed be your name.
Your kingdom come,
Your will be done in earth, as it is in heaven.
Give us this day our daily bread.
And forgive us our debts, as
we forgive our debtors.
And lead us not into temptation, but deliver
us from evil: For yours is the kingdom, and
the power, and the glory, forever. Amen."

- Matt: 6:9-13

Samba sat in his study as the night wore on. He was increasingly facing the reality that his father, who had been a larger-than-life figure in his life, was living out his last days. As he drowned one cup of coffee after another, he resolved to make some changes in his life and conduct. He resolved not to run for political office, not this time, no matter what the implications would be. He was going to listen to one voice. "The voice of truth," he called it. He felt a little bitter towards his father and his effect on him and yet he knew that as his father, Jabali More, had done some good as well. Lately, Samba had assisted his father in several attempts to correct some of his mistakes and these attempts had made the headlines.

While some thought that Jabali More was genuine in his repentance and actions, some considered him a hypocrite. Some lawyers and human rights activists had indicated that the likes of Jabali More should face imprisonment and not admiration. They wished that he would recover and pay for the damage he had done to the public. *Forgiveness is bending one's back one more time knowing well the risk of having the offender ride on it; without the power to get rid of the offender, nor the power to prevent the offense. It is difficult to escape one's own family and forgiving is a better option than bitterness,* Samba thought.

It had been a while since he saw Pastor Noel. He decided to call him the next day and request him for a short after work meeting; a cup of coffee and he would apologise for trying to bribe him. Soon after making these resolutions, Samba's heart settled in a quiet peace which felt quite alien and yet pleasant to him. It was already 4am and wrapping himself in a shawl, he slid in his chair and dosed off. Natasha had been exhausted the previous night and had gone to bed by 10pm, before he had arrived at the house. At 6:30am, he woke up and took a quick shower in the little bathroom located downstairs, not wanting to disturb Natasha. He went to the kitchen to prepare some breakfast for both of them and take it upstairs to their room. He couldn't wait to tell Natasha what he had decided.

Natasha ate her breakfast as Samba mostly spoke and poured out his heart to her. "Considering what you did last time, I'm afraid, Noel might not be that willing to see you without an appointment Samba," she said. "Let me help you out. I will make the call for you and convince him to see you."

"Baby, that will be quite okay," Samba replied, feeling grateful and relieved. She later called Pastor Noel and her effort was successful. She arranged a meeting for the two at a warm, intimate coffee house.

*****

Later that evening, Pastor Noel Karo was driving home after his coffee meeting with Samba More when his eye caught the outline of what seemed to be a woman seated by the roadside, rather precariously, leaning her back on the trunk of a tree. As he slowed down, he recognised the orange-brown headscarf on her head. It seemed quite familiar. He slowed down and pulled over to the side of the road and sure enough, the woman recognised him before he had a chance to say hello.

"Pastor Noel!" she said weakly.

Noel looked at the woman recalling her name. It was a lonely spot in between the city, along the route leading to Sabuni slum where Salome resided.

"Salome what are you doing here at the side of the road at this hour of evening? Don't you know it's getting dangerous by the minute?"

There were some trees lining the side of the road and the place was a dangerous mugging spot in the late evenings and during the night. It was already 5 o'clock in the evening.

"Pastor I have walked all the way from town and I am feeling a little weak. I do not have bus fare to get me home," she answered.

"Please come in quickly Salome," he said without hesitation, opening the door for her.

She dragged herself up from the tuft of grass she had sat

on, and got into the car. Pastor Noel fiddled with the steering wheel as he thought of what could have become of this woman. He had not seen her for over a year. The cars sped by, this being a somewhat lonely spot along the route as he waited for a chance to get back on the road. He had some soft drinks in the car which he had bought for his daughter and his son. He reached the back seat and pulled out one of these, handing it to her.

"So how are you Salome, where have you been?" he asked lightly.

"I am fine Pastor," Salome said, her head bowing as she stared at the drink in her laps. Her eyes were tired and vacant. "I am just very tired but I have been living as you advised me to although my work is still not as good. I am doing small jobs for different people and have not yet been employed."

He tried to engage Salome in some small talk as he drove onto the road and continued with the journey, but it didn't seem forthcoming. The car became silent as the sound of a song coming from his car radio dominated. Soon, the outline of a sprawling satellite settlement came into view. They arrived at a bus stop along the route and Pastor Noel handed Salome a five hundred shillings note and advised her to take a bus that will drop her at her house.

"Thank you Pastor. I feel much better now. I will come to the office to see you." she said and left.

Pastor Noel took a turn that would lead him to his home and drove on. It was a busy evening as Sherry and Noel engaged the children as they did their homework and during dinner. Later when the children were in bed, Noel told Sherry about his encounter with Samba and his apology.

"That's wonderful news Noel," Sherry remarked. "Let's give him a chance, after all we are already linked in some ways and Natasha is a wonderful person."

"Yeah, all in all, Samba is not too bad as an individual either," Noel agreed.

*****

Two months had gone by when at 7:30am one morning, after finishing a quick breakfast in preparation for the early morning service to begin at 8am, Noel got a call from Samba.

"Good morning Samba," he greeted him.

"Good morning," Samba replied urgently.

"Is everything okay?" he inquired.

"Not really Pastor Noel, dad passed on half an hour ago," he said.

"Oh, I am so sorry," Pastor Noel said, "I was just about to leave for church but will have to call the church and tell them to excuse me and that I will be in for the other service instead."

After Pastor Noel arrived at Jabali More's residence, he prayed with the gathered family members and the body was taken to the mortuary. He then went back to the house at about 10am and had a change of clothes and a cup of tea and left for the second church service that begun at 10:30am.

*****

Church members held prayers at Jabali More's residence until the date for the burial arrived.

*****

Samba stood by his father's ornate casket. It was made of steel, was painted white and gold plated at the edges. Everything

161

about the funeral was expensive. Samba looked around at those who stood by and the attendees. Although his father's political friends were in attendance along with their relatives, mostly the well to do, he couldn't quite point out even one man who stood out as an admirable figure. There was none of them who possessed the kind of character traits that he admired on a personal level. They may be rich, privileged and complicated but lacking in pure traits of kindness and love, kindness without the taint of self interest.

He had no doubt that his father had the qualities of a natural leader and no doubt he had begun well. However, as he grew wealthier and more powerful, he had become a different man. He had especially been afraid of death and seemed to be haunted by some things he had done. On Samba's right hand stood Pastor Noel Karo, a great relief to him. His late father would not have had it any other way. During his lifetime, Samba's father, Jabali More, had not seen eye to eye with Rev. Jay Karo, Pastor Noel's father, on several issues. At the time of Rev. Jay's death, they had not spoken with each other for almost five years only to connect again a few months before his passing on. He had been aware that his son Samba attended Woodlands City Congregation many times and Natasha, his daughter-in-law, was a member at this church. On this occasion, Samba felt safe and reassured by Pastor Noel Karo and his staff's presence.

In the last few months before his demise, Jabali More's health had deteriorated. Liver failure had caught up with his system. He was not a drunkard, but had drunk habitually during his lifetime, preferring wine and strong spirits to beer. When his health was failing, Jabali More had begun asking after Rev. Jay's son, Pastor Noel Karo, and how he was fairing.

His son Samba was quick to narrate the details of Pastor Noel Karo's struggles in the past few years culminating in the loss of church members, his sacrifice, near poverty and now strong re-emergence.

In the hot afternoons during the difficult period of his convalescence, Jabali More recalled many details of his life, both the highlights and low moments. It seemed that the low moments were the defining moments of his life. Dozing in the shade, he would catch a nap and dream and suddenly he would be back at home in the coastal village, biting into ripe tropical mangoes, cracking coconuts, catching tadpoles, walking on the pure and bare beaches and swimming in the gigantic Indian ocean when the tide wasn't too high and scary. He would dream of fishing as a child and how the laughter would ring during their adventures with Jay Karo, his childhood friend, besides him. They had been friends until they each grew up to follow different paths, never losing touch with each other but growing farther and farther apart as each pursued their own set of ideals. If he was going to die, he needed a friend on the other side. Some of his contemporaries had passed on in recent years but he wasn't as sure that he would like it if they would be the ones to meet him on the other side. But if it were Jay... if it were Rev. Jay Karo, everything would be okay and if Andrea followed after it would be all the better. It was at this time that Jabali More started asking after Rev. Jay's son, Noel. He had attended Rev. Jay Karo's funeral and had visited him a couple of times before his time of ailing, when he had been diagnosed with prostate cancer.

Pastor Noel Karo had prayed with him many times. Jabali didn't know quite why but he always felt better after they had prayed. Pastor Noel Karo seemed quite brilliant, even when it came to political thought and inclinations, and therefore he enjoyed chatting with him. It was amazing how his thoughts remained clean. Jabali had known many dirty tricks and at the height of his political career, he could force almost anything to go his way sometimes. Pastor Noel had spoken to him about asking God for forgiveness. Forgiveness was something that made him admit his guilt and his weakness. Jabali was accustomed to pay, bribe or force his way through using whatever means necessary, especially money. However, Pastor Noel wouldn't accept any money from him. He would come and go at his own cost. Jabali knew that even if Pastor Noel accepted the money; it wouldn't have necessarily meant that God had forgiven him.

In the end, Jabali More had prayed and confessed that he was a sinner at the end of his rope. *Even the best of men make many mistakes in life as their humanity, their weakness, trips them every now and then and they too fall. I have done some good in my life but I have also perpetrated evil in many ways, setting a twisted standard in political conduct and causing many innocent people to suffer.* He had thought.

Noel Karo had told him, "Forgiveness is the dawning of a new day when the night is past. It is acknowledgement that yesterday; the sun did set and today is the result."

Samba had felt that his life, which afforded him much of everything that he had wanted, was but night; his soul had continually been darkened. Here was something that money couldn't buy! He would be stupid to refuse the offer of forgiveness.

There on his bed in his last days, Jabali had asked God to forgive him of the crooked path he had trod. He knew he may not have the ability to right all the wrongs in his life, but yet

164

he felt a weight lifting off his shoulders even as he prayed. His countenance also appeared brighter and more peaceful than before. In the last two months before his death, Jabali More had sought forgiveness from his family members and wider circle of colleagues and friends whom he had wronged. He especially asked for forgiveness from two families who had suffered loss of the family's breadwinners as a result of his direct orders to his goons to beat the two men in order to silence them and teach them a lesson. The two had been activists who had come across evidence that implicated him and his son Samba in a corrupt government procurement deal that had resulted in the loss of hundreds of millions of shillings of public money. The goons he had relied on to do his dirty job and get rid of the collected evidence if possible, had instead beaten the two activists to death. A remorseful, teary, yet composed Jabali had asked the widows of the two men to forgive him for his actions and the suffering that had ensued after the demise of their husbands. After much persuasion through a middle man, the widows had acceded to his request that he establishes a trust fund for the education of their children and provide each widow with a quarter acre piece of land.

During the last month of his life, Jabali had improved tremendously from his illness and had managed to attend to minor tasks as well as to attend Sunday church services where Pastor Noel Karo preached. His family members had hosted one party with few guests to cheer him up and wish him further recovery. However, one rainy Sunday morning when he had already worn his white shirt and royal blue jacket, ready to attend the early service at Woodlands City Congregation, the house help had found him seated as if in a daze at the breakfast table. He had had poured himself some hot coffee and sat back, probably to peruse the newspaper on the table and proceed to down his coffee just like in old times, but it was not to be.

To her dismay, the house help had realised that Jabali More was long gone. He had been silent for at least ten minutes when she had last heard his voice asking for his toast just like in old times. He had not had toast since when he had been diagnosed with liver failure among other complications. *God is gracious, who would have thought Jabali More would get a second chance to life?* she had thought.

*****

There were no flowers at Jabali More's funeral. He had made this last request to his son during the days he felt weakest during his convalescence. As much as he knew that he had repented of his sin and was accepted by God, he felt the need to avert unnecessary attention and expenditure during his funeral. Omitting flowers was one of the things he had requested as well as only the presence of key family friends and colleagues where he would be put to rest finally at their farm in the Rift Valley. However, anyone who wished to could attend the church service in the city.

*****

Sheba Shilishoi hurried to fit into her white cotton and lace dress in order to go and attend the funeral. Samba's wife, Natasha was counting on her to be there. Eric was ready and waiting for her in the living room. She walked out of the room in her white dress which fit tighter than usual. *How did I put on this weight?* she thought to herself and gathered her handbag to walk out of the house and into the car. Her hair was tied in a ponytail at the back and she wore pale pink lipstick, eyeliner and low heeled black suede shoes. Sheba had chosen white for the funeral as opposed to black. George Mumbai once told her that in her rural area it was the custom for people to wear white as opposed to black during funerals, especially those who were Christians. This signified the passage into another life and hope. Sheba knew that Jabali More had changed before his death and it was fitting for her to think of hope at his funeral. George, Natasha and Sherry had also worn white dresses in varied designs.

*****

Although Samba and Natasha's large family were present, they were especially comforted by the presence of their Christian friends. Eric and Sheba were seated directly behind them during the short service at their farm. Eric and Sheba had left Nairobi very early and had reached the More's home in exactly two hours. The neighbouring villagers had turned up despite the plea that only family and close friends should attend. It was a very hot day and the sun shone overhead. Sheba had a bottle of water in her hand which she sipped as she began to feel a little dizzy. As they walked to the grave site and the casket was lowered into the earth, Sheba suddenly felt an upsurge of nausea and instinctively moved through the crowd, leaving Eric still standing stalwart besides Samba. A distance away from the activities, a short shrub beckoned and she suddenly began throwing up continuously. For close to two minutes. Feeling slightly frustrated and infuriated, she recalled asking her house help Mimo not to spice up the eggs in the morning but to her dismay, Mimo had done exactly that. Eric had insisted on spices when she had gone into the bathroom to take her bath. She usually experienced slight nausea during travel and preferred to eat a simple meal or not at all depending on the distance and means of travel.

Noticing her plight, a young farmhand came with a spade of loose earth and covered the vomit.

"*Asante sana*, thank you very much," Sheba said to the lad. Taking a sip of water, she quietly went back to where her husband was standing as they sung the last hymn: *When the Roll is Called Up Yonder*. Sheba and Natasha hugged each other. George Mumbai and Sherry Karo drew close to Natasha and hugged her as well.

Lunch was served as Samba's family received condolences from those who had attended. At 6pm, Eric and Sheba, Sherry and Pastor Noel Karo, George and Michael Mumbai and their families bid the family goodbye and started on their journey back to Nairobi. Eusebia and Mimo had remained in Nairobi this time in order to rest a little, since they too had been involved in serving people at the More's home since his demise. The group reached Nairobi at 9pm and went to their homes exhausted.

The next day, Sheba got up before Eric and got ready. Eric dragged himself out of bed and into the living room just as she was about to leave for the hospital.

"Where to this early honey?" he asked.

"I'm going to the hospital to be checked Eric," she answered.

"I don't feel well since yesterday and with the weather changes, I don't want to come down with something," she answered.

"I am coming with you," he said.

"No it's okay, let me just go, I'll be fine. Besides, you're still in your pyjamas and..." Eric had disappeared into the bedroom and he came out in a t-shirt and jeans.

"Let's go," he said, snatching her car keys from her. "I'll drive!" Sheba resigned to the turn of events and meekly sat at the passenger seat of her car as her husband drove to their family doctor's practice.

"I wanted to catch him before he leaves for Nairobi hospital at 9am," she intimated. Most doctors usually had a clinic which they operated in addition to where they were employed. They got to the clinic in good time and after exchanging pleasantries with the doctor, Sheba got to describing how she had been feeling for the past one week. She suspected that she was experiencing the symptoms similar to those which one has when undergoing menopause, since she had missed her period for the second consecutive month. However, she hadn't expected to undergo menopause at a fairly early stage in her life for she was turning forty-five. .

"Okay Sheba, let's get down to business and run some tests on you," the doctor stated.

She went to the laboratory and a number of tests were conducted on her. Thirty minutes later the doctor emerged from the laboratory and proceeded to his office. Shortly after, the receptionist requested Sheba and Eric to go into the doctor's office. They went in and sat facing the doctor who was beaming with a smile.

"Sheba, I am glad to inform you that you are perfectly healthy and not even undergoing menopause as you had suspected," the doctor began.

"Then what could the matter be?" Sheba inquired quizzically. Her forehead was creasing as she leaned on her husband's arm.

"Sheba and Eric, I am glad to be the one to let you know that after all these years and all these struggles, God has answered your prayers. Sheba, you are finally pregnant!" he announced.

Sheba let out a slight scream while Eric looked at the doctor with bated breath and turned to his wife and hugged her tightly.

"You are two months pregnant Sheba," the doctor continued.

Sheba bowed her head in silent prayer and yet she couldn't say much as tears streamed down her face. Her heart was dancing in both joy and disbelief. "God is faithful," she murmured.

When they walked out of the clinic, it was as if they were in a dream.

"Let's say a prayer of thanksgiving before we leave this place," Eric said.

They bowed down and he prayed a short prayer of thanksgiving.

"We must call our closest friends who have been praying with us concerning this day and share with them the good news," Eric said. Sheba got into the house and took her mobile phone and began making calls to her close friends. She called Natasha More, Sherry Karo and George Mumbai.

"Something very good and very exciting has happened and Eric and I want you to come with your spouse so that we can make the announcement and thank God together," she said.

Out of curiosity and excitement at the tone of Sheba's voice, all her three friends agreed to drop by at their house for dinner with their spouses that evening. Though it was early in the day, Mimo took Sheba's instructions and promptly began preparing for dinner.

Sheba was especially delighted since Pastor Noel Karo doubled both as a friend and their pastor. She wanted them to have joint prayer concerning the months ahead. Although Eric didn't like shopping, he gladly went to the supermarket to get some additional groceries which were needed for that evening.

At exactly 6:30pm Natasha and Samba More drove into Sheba's compound. A year ago, they had bought a house with a large compound, moving out of the apartment they had lived in for quite a while which had been large and comfortable too. Sheba hadn't wanted them to move into their own house with a compound citing loneliness since they would be enclosed and it would therefore be difficult to hear the sound of the neighbour's children and other sounds from those around them. However, with some persuasion from Eric, she had conceded that they should buy their own house and not a larger flat since they often hosted a wide range of visitors at their premises. It was a beautiful house.

*****

Pastor Noel and Sherry Karo followed afterwards and then Michael and George Mumbai. Sheba's sister also came. The music was playing and the front door was open to receive the visitors. Sheba welcomed the visitors into the house as Mimo and her sister served everyone with drinks of their choice. Being a Saturday evening, Sheba knew it would be important to end the evening by 9pm since the following day was Sunday and it held responsibilities for all of them, especially Pastor Noel and Sherry Karo.

At 7:30pm, dinner was served and they ate as the discussion moved from one topic to another. There was an evident build up of suspense as Mimo and Sheba's sister took the dishes away and prepared to serve them dessert.

"C'mon Sheba, this suspense is killing me," Sherry blurted out and they all laughed out heartily as the rest agreed that it really was time to tell the good news.

"Okay, my friends," Eric began, "We have been praying together for quite a number of years now and I know you have continually prayed for us in the privacy of your chambers as well. Sheba and I would like to let you know that today itself, we found out that God has been gracious to answer our prayers. Sheba has been a little under the weather for this past one week. We visited our doctor today morning and instead of an ailment, we were delighted to find out that Sheba is two months pregnant. We're pregnant!" he announced.

There was a chorus of ohh and ahh as the ladies - George, Natasha and Sherry stood from their chairs and went round the table to hug their dear friend Sheba. The men stood from their chairs and gave Eric a hug too.

"Congratulations man!" Pastor Noel Karo said as he patted Eric's back. "Isn't God faithful?"

The men each congratulated Sheba as well, kissing her on the cheek. The women retreated to a section of the living room to inquire more details from Sheba, asking her for the fine details of her discovery and the men were making jokes as they rejoiced with Eric.

"I was wondering if you perhaps had some friends and relatives visiting when I saw that baby cot which seems functional and decorated there at the corner." Natasha exclaimed.

"I put it there as a symbolic gesture," Sheba answered.

Mimo approached Sheba and informed her that dessert was already served. "Okay, ladies and gentlemen, let's go back to the table please, dessert and coffee is served."

They went and sat at the table. It was interesting to note how pleasantly different Samba More could be when he felt he was in the right company.

*****

The clock chimed 9pm and Eric asked Pastor Noel if they would have a short session of prayer before they left for their homes. Pastor Noel quickly requested that they move to the seating area and there Sheba and Eric would kneel and they would surround them in a circle and pray over them and the new pregnancy. The friends all prayed concerning Sheba and Eric's pregnancy and Pastor Noel Karo concluded with a final prayer. As they left the Mureithi's home, the ladies had already planned a separate time to get together and meet to advise and offer any assistance that Sheba might need.

*****

"God's goodness is tangible," Pastor Noel said to his wife as they got into bed to sleep. He gently pushed strands of hair away from her face "It is obvious to anyone who's looking."

*****

The Sunday service went on well as scheduled and Pastor Noel and Sherry took their children Miriam and John out for lunch and swimming as they also enjoyed their lunch and each other's company.

Pastor Noel took this opportunity to inform Sherry that Teresa, a church member, trained in Bible studies would be starting Swahili services at Woodlands City Congregation to commence at 7am every Sunday and end at 8:30 am. She would be assisted by Eugene and Simon. Due to that, the other two English services would be rearranged and pushed to 9am and 11am respectively to accommodate this new development. Many members who were more comfortable in Kiswahili would be accommodated in this service and perhaps more with similar inclinations could join. Sherry was happy to hear about it and informed her husband that the last payment towards the exhibition they had had amounted to about four million Kenyan shillings or fifty thousand US dollars and was expected during the next week. Although the money from the Sunday tithes and offerings and the art exhibition was coming in slowly, the Woodlands City Congregation was steadily heading towards completion of the painting, other fittings, fixtures and finer details. Recently, the number of people had started growing steadily again.

Chapter 11

❋

Apostle Francis shuddered at the thought of what was to come to pass, if indeed it would happen. He was troubled in his inner person with how far he would wade into the macabre activities demanded of him by "Master". Initially, he had maintained the fake demeanour of a church minister by sheer manipulation, trickery and a mastery of sections of the Bible and how to twist it.

His initial goal was to simply make some money and get rich if possible. However, he had found it difficult to exit from the path he had started treading. A fellow masquerading as a church minister as well had introduced him to the more unscrupulous methods of the underworld which though unpleasant, left him without the need to depend on his congregation for funds but rather made matters easier or so it seemed. After visiting Master, instead of hiring people to act and pretend that they were healed, he seemed to have the ability to effect an actual healing or financial breakthrough when he faked a prayer for those affected. The people also seemed to be under some spell and gave out their money easier.

He was introduced to a powerful occult practitioner who provided charms of all kinds to his clients, some of whom were really powerful members of society. The occultist was known as Master and had dedicated himself to the devil and freely informed and warned those who sought his help that they too would be servants to the evil being known as Satan and would have to pay a price for the good life they wanted to live, even with other people's lives if need be.

Apostle Francis had planned to get a mild charm from this person but he had noted the effect the charm he obtained had on his church business. More people had flocked into the Assembly of Wonders and End Day Miracles and he had to admit that he was not only addicted to money but power as well. He had enjoyed his undue influence over the people. Shortly after, some financial problems had cropped up when he had decided to expand his facilities and at the same time purchase the latest model of a range rover. His funds had suddenly dried up and he seemed to be in a desert. The shortage of funds and desperation had sent him to Master once again. He was to find out that as his need grew so did his dependence on this figure, Master.

He was fast getting entangled in a web that he was starting to hate, having enjoyed freedom to do as he wished previously. He could hardly believe that on this day, he, Apostle Francis, would deliver members of his congregation to death by way of a road accident and remain the sole survivor after the accident. This would be his final dealing with the Master.

He had been told not to worry himself with details and questions on how the accident would take place. Master would see to it that it certainly took place. "It will be fatal, fatal," the Master had said to him but only you will survive. Apostle Francis had to admit that he could no longer be classified as an innocent person at all and that he hardly got scared but nevertheless, the kind of thing he was going to do was more than he had ever wanted to be involved in. As he listened to the Master's weird voice, he felt a slight sickness at the pit of his stomach. A voice at the far end of his conscience suggested that he should perhaps quit this deal while there was still time but another voice urged him on, since this would be a final deal for him anyway.

With him in the van, among others, was his assistant pastor. It had been three years since Peter had joined his team.

"That cursed woman Salome never made it here," Apostle Francis muttered to himself. *Though the woman seems to be a little more self-aware and self-controlled lately, she is still largely an idiot, worthless scum, and it wouldn't be much damage if the society lost her,* he thought. *I wonder what Pastor Noel Karo has that makes him the success that he is and why he didn't succumb even when he was at his worst,* he marvelled.

*****

Salome had received an urgent call from her neighbour on her way to Assembly of Wonders and End Day Miracles church compound and had to return to her house and attend to her child. Her child, who was asthmatic, suffered most attacks during the cold season of the year and would sometimes be critical. Although Salome had returned to worship at Woodlands City Congregation and had acquired some friends like Eusebia and Mimo among others, she had agreed to accompany Apostle Francis on his mission trip to Turkana upon his requesting her to do so. Salome had fallen prey to her ego and feeling a sense of importance when asked to accompany Apostle Francis who she thought despised her, was flattering.

By the time she returned to the church compound to inquire whether the van had already left, she was informed that it indeed had left about an hour ago and that it was too late. Apostle Francis and his team continued on with the journey to Turkana, taking the Nairobi – Nakuru highway moving steadily, aiming to go to Kitale where they would proceed to Lodwar.

*****

Maria had gotten up early to go and fetch firewood from the nearby bush. At the back of her mind, she was aware that it was already three weeks into the school term and her children had missed some lessons. Nevertheless she was concerned with survival when she left, disturbed by the sheer terror of the discovery she had made.

She had made some *mandazis*[14] for the children and some black tea. Her little ones stirred awake and she welcomed them for a cup of tea. Their great grandmother was still asleep in her bedroom. Maria switched on the little radio to a local fm station in order to listen to the morning news and some gospel music. They were midway into their breakfast when the news came on. As usual, politics was centre stage and there were highlights of the rains that were wreaking havoc in some areas of the country. Suddenly, Maria froze with another bite into the fleshy pastry and increased the volume of her little radio. She had heard Apostle Francis name and then right afterwards she had heard her husband's name - Peter Maranga. The church - Assembly of Wonders and End Day Miracles - was also mentioned. They had been involved in a grisly accident along the highway and there was no survivor left. The news stated that all fourteen passengers in the minivan which had the logo of the church and were reportedly on a mission trip to Turkana region had perished when the van had been involved in a head on collision with an oncoming lorry.

Maria sunk into her chair in fear and disbelief. Her husband had died and she had heard it on the news. *What*

14   Soft pastry made of wheat, Swahili origin.

should I do now? Should I remain in hiding or should I go and get involved in the burial rites? she thought. She decided to ask her grandmother for advise when she woke up. The children had finished their breakfast and had proceeded to play outside; totally unaware of what had just taken place.

At about 8:30am, her grandmother woke up and washed her face and sat down for breakfast.

"Mueni," grandmother said, "You are looking disturbed, is there anything wrong?"

"Grandma, you already know why I am here and what Peter became," she began.

"I know that, do you feel you can confront him now?" she inquired.

"No grandma. Today in the news, I heard an announcement and it was the death of my husband and Apostle Francis Katana. They were travelling with twelve other passengers who also died. There were no survivors grandma, Peter is dead!" she answered.

Her grandmother sat still in silence for some time.

"It would have been good if Peter had lived to repent but who knows, maybe he would become worse and so God knows best. I know this might sound callous my child but yet in one way or another, God has answered your prayer. You will now be able to continue with your life in peace without any obligation to your husband who had chosen to serve Satan. You belong to God and you will serve Jesus Christ and so will your children," grandmother said.

"Yes grandma, you are right," Maria answered. She had mixed feelings about what had happened. When she married Peter, he had been such a wonderful man who loved God, and though he was poor, she had faith that together they would be successful and build a beautiful family and something tangible to call their own. Before Peter started the religious delusions that led to his connection with Apostle Francis, he had been doing well, running a small retail, corner shop. It was true that she felt some relief that her problem was solved but yet there was a deep sadness she felt; that she would ever have had a connection with a man who turned out to be evil.

"Grandma, should I attend Peter's funeral or should I remain in hiding?" she asked.

"It's going to be hard, but I feel that you should attend the funeral," grandmother began. "A dead man will not be able to harm you and since his family did not know what he was up to, if you fail to attend his funeral, it would be difficult to convince them that you did not harbour ill will against your husband when he was alive. For now, you will offer the simple explanation that the two of you had a misunderstanding and you felt that you needed to separate from him for a while. You can be assured that God will protect you as he has protected you until now.

Your mother and her prayer group, as well as I will pray for you and the children."

Maria Mueni listened to her grandmother and felt that it was sound advice. She prepared to leave the remote hills of Masii and travel to the city and brace herself for the funeral. She would go with her mother and three women from her prayer group and one of their pastors. They would stay with her during the funeral preparations and the subsequent burial. More of her relatives and friends would join her later.

Maria arrived at the flat they were staying in, the following day at noon and found the house help busy serving lunch.

Peter's mother and father, his brother and uncle had arrived from the village. A small group from the Assembly of Wonders and End Day Miracles had also come to give their condolences. A week of funeral preparations went on. Peter's family members had travelled to participate as well.

Peter's parents were Seventh Day Adventists and were ordinary folk; hard workers engaged in an honest livelihood most of their lives. They also had the fear of God and steadfastly served in their local church. All their children had grown up to be responsible adults engaged in good careers especially the first two children, one of whom was a doctor and another who was a secondary school teacher. The other three included a kindergarten teacher, a mechanic and Peter, their last born, who had been a small scale business man and later a Pastor.

Peter's parents insisted that the funeral should be done by the Seventh Day Adventist church and since Apostle Francis wasn't alive to protest, the junior pastors left behind at Assembly of Wonders and End Day Miracles had agreed to it. Maria Mueni Maranga, the widow, had resorted to go through the funeral quietly and afterwards, she would begin her life afresh, away from the Assembly of Wonders and End Day Miracles as well as its members. One week after her husband's demise, they travelled to their rural home and there they conducted the funeral service. Maria's brother had remained in Nairobi to find a cheap house where she could move in and start a new life. Having run her grocery business all through, she had saved some money and she had decided to take nothing that had belonged to both of them with her to the new house. Custom required that a widow should stay on for a little while after her husband's burial and Maria fulfilled this condition as well. She stayed on with the children and her mother for the next one week. On returning to Nairobi, she went straight to the house that her brother had rented and organised on her behalf.

*****

Pastor Noel Karo got a phone call from Apophia, the village woman who informed her that Papa, his grandfather, had passed on in his sleep the previous night. "Oh grandpa," Noel sighed. Due to his age, he wasn't very shocked or very sad either but he would miss him for sure. He called up his siblings and cousins and they quickly made arrangements to converge at their home at the Coast for the funeral by the following day. Since the coast was about 600km away from Nairobi, some of them took flights as others travelled by road. The date of burial was coinciding with the date that Apostle Francis of Assembly of Wonders and End Day Miracles was to be buried. The leadership of Woodlands City Congregation as well as the Mumbai's, More's and Mureithi's travelled all the way for the burial of Mwalimu Karo. Some members of Woodlands City Congregation travelled all the way too including Salome who helped with the domestic work. Sheba left her little infant in her sister's care and promptly returned the following day on an early morning flight.

*****

The local church did most of the singing and the preaching was done by Mwalimu Karo's pastor as well. There were a lot of traditional flutes and shakers known as *kayamba* as well as an instrument known as *marimba*, a form of the xylophone. The songs were Christian but with adapted traditional sound renditions.

*****

Maria Mueni Maranga, Peter's widow, had taken approximately three years to recover completely from her grief and trauma. Initially, she had had terrible nightmares after the burial of her husband. Many times she would dream of being back in the Assembly of Wonders and End Day Miracles and on such nights she woke up and prayed concerning the dream especially since she had vowed to never again set foot in that church. She usually spent her Sunday mornings in the house watching services on Christian television. It took eight months for her to muster courage to set foot into the door of another church. She decided to try attending services at Woodlands City Congregation. She had heard some good reports about the church from credible people. Her own brother had attended Sunday services there for the month he had spent at her house immediately after the death of her husband.

It was at Woodlands City Congregation that she discovered a beneficial programme to her. Woodlands City Congregation had come up with a spiritual counselling programme for people who had undergone tough spiritual experiences that left them scarred and in shock in the process of what was known as spiritual warfare in Christianity. This was after realising the need, especially, after George's extended time of bizarre spiritual experiences. Factors like fear of being alone immediately after a period of prolonged warfare experiences or mistrusting spiritual leaders, for those who had encounters such as those Maria had, were handled and counselees equipped on how to overcome and regain a balanced and positive outlook in life again. The pastor in the programme remind counselees of the fact that not even Jesus Christ had been exempted from tough spiritual experiences, while citing Matthew chapter four and emphasising that after such experiences there is growth, victory and relief as was his case both during this time and after his crucifixion and resurrection (Matt. 4:11 - *Then the devil left him, and angels came and attended him.* Luk. 22:43 - *An angel from heaven appeared to him and strengthened him*). Maria became a regular attendant at the church, electing to go to the Swahili services run by Pastor Teresa and her team.

*****

One day, as she sat in her living room with her children watching the news, there was a news item about Assembly of Wonders and End Day Miracles. The church was featured as having gone bankrupt and all the property in the name of the church having been auctioned. A bulldozer was shown tearing into the building rendering everything flat and useless. The developer was going to put up new structures for a factory venture. Though she knew that false pastors and false churches still exist, this particular outcome gave her further relief and closure.

*****

It was the month of February, one Sunday when the congregation was least expecting, the ushers directed them to the new church building. The pastors had requested members to come with visitors during the next Sunday but hadn't told them that the new auditorium would be inaugurated and dedicated. It therefore came as a pleasant surprise. They now understood why it had taken a large amount of money to build the sanctuary. The fittings and fixtures were of a high quality and the acoustics and sound system were excellent. The finishing was great and the seats comfortable. It had been five years since they had broken ground for the building activities to begin. Five years of great lessons. The auditorium was large, with a capacity to seat seven thousand. There were visitors officially invited by the church leadership and older ministers. Pastor Seth who was now pastor to a smaller church was also in attendance. The downstairs part of the building was filled but the upper part was empty except for a few adventurous people who had opted to sit there. Eusebia was among those who sat upstairs with her daughter Rose who had come to live with her and go to university.

That night Noel slept soundly as he was very tired. Several songs and pictures of the Woodlands City Congregation's re-launch ran through his mind in a dream. Briefly he saw the face of his father, the late Rev. Jay Karo, and almost heard a few strains of music. Was it his father's childhood song "*Nakupenda Kama Sukari*"?

Hymns

Great is Thy Faithfulness

Great is Thy faithfulness, O God my Father;
There is no shadow of turning with Thee;
Thou changest not, Thy compassions, they fail not;
As Thou hast been, Thou forever will be.

Refrain
Great is Thy faithfulness!
Great is Thy faithfulness!
Morning by morning new mercies I see.
All I have needed Thy hand hath provided;
Great is Thy faithfulness, Lord, unto me!

Summer and winter and springtime and harvest,
Sun, moon and stars in their courses above
Join with all nature in manifold witness
To Thy great faithfulness, mercy and love.

Refrain

Pardon for sin and a peace that endureth
Thine own dear presence to cheer and to guide;
Strength for today and bright hope for tomorrow,
Blessings all mine, with ten thousand beside!

Refrain

We're Marching to Zion

Come, we that love the Lord,
And let our joys be known;
Join in a song with sweet accord,
Join in a song with sweet accord
And thus surround the throne,
And thus surround the throne.

Refrain
We're marching to Zion,
Beautiful, beautiful Zion;
We're marching upward to Zion,
The beautiful city of God.

The sorrows of the mind
Be banished from the place;
Religion never was designed
Religion never was designed,
To make our pleasures less,
To make our pleasures less.

Refrain

Let those refuse to sing,
Who never knew our God;
But favorites of the heavenly King,
But favorites of the heavenly King
May speak their joys abroad,
May speak their joys abroad.

Refrain

Sell Me a Prayer

The God that rules on high,
And thunders when He please,
Who rides upon the stormy sky,
Who rides upon the stormy sky,
And manages the seas,
And manages the seas.

Refrain

This awful God is ours,
Our Father and our Love;
He will send down his heav'nly powers,
He will send down his heav'nly powers,
To carry us above,
To carry us above.

Refrain

There we shall see His face,
And never, never sin!
There, from the rivers of His grace,
There, from the rivers of His grace,
Drink endless pleasures in,
Drink endless pleasures in.

Refrain

Yea, and before we rise,
To that immortal state,
The thoughts of such amazing bliss,
The thoughts of such amazing bliss,
Should constant joys create,
Should constant joys create.

189

Refrain

The men of grace have found,
Glory begun below.
Celestial fruits on earthly ground
Celestial fruits on earthly ground
From faith and hope may grow,
From faith and hope may grow.

Refrain

The hill of Zion yields
A thousand sacred sweets
Before we reach the heav'nly fields,
Before we reach the heav'nly fields,
Or walk the golden streets,
Or walk the golden streets.

Refrain

Then let our songs abound,
And every tear be dry;
We're marching through Immanuel's ground,
We're marching through Immanuel's ground,
To fairer worlds on high,
To fairer worlds on high.

Refrain

Rock of Ages, Cleft for Me

Rock of Ages, cleft for me,
Let me hide myself in Thee;
Let the water and the blood,
From Thy wounded side which flowed,
Be of sin the double cure;
Save from wrath and make me pure.

Not the labor of my hands
Can fulfill Thy law's demands;
Could my zeal no respite know,
Could my tears forever flow,
All for sin could not atone;
Thou must save, and Thou alone.

Nothing in my hand I bring,
Simply to the cross I cling;
Naked, come to Thee for dress;
Helpless look to Thee for grace;
Foul, I to the fountain fly;
Wash me, Savior, or I die.

While I draw this fleeting breath,
When mine eyes shall close in death,
[*originally* When my eye-strings break in death]
When I soar to worlds unknown,
See Thee on Thy judgment throne,
Rock of Ages, cleft for me,
Let me hide myself in Thee.

About the Author

Sheila Bosire is a publisher and editor as well as an author who has written a number of children's books and adult literature including *Mama is Sweet, The Giant Lollipop Tree, The Strongest Father, My Century at the Kenyan Coast* among others. She also runs a magazine blog - *www.beliefmagazine.wordpress.com* for the periodical magazine *Belief.*

She is a born again Christian with a passion for faith matters, Christian service and ecumenism. *Sell Me a Prayer* is her first novel in the African Christian fiction category. She holds a Bachelor's degree in Literature and Sociology from Kenyatta University class of 2003 and has recently studied Politics and International Relations at Mumbai University.

www.ingramcontent.com/pod-product-compliance
Lightning Source LLC
Chambersburg PA
CBHW060400030726
47497CB00003B/792